STAND ON GRACE

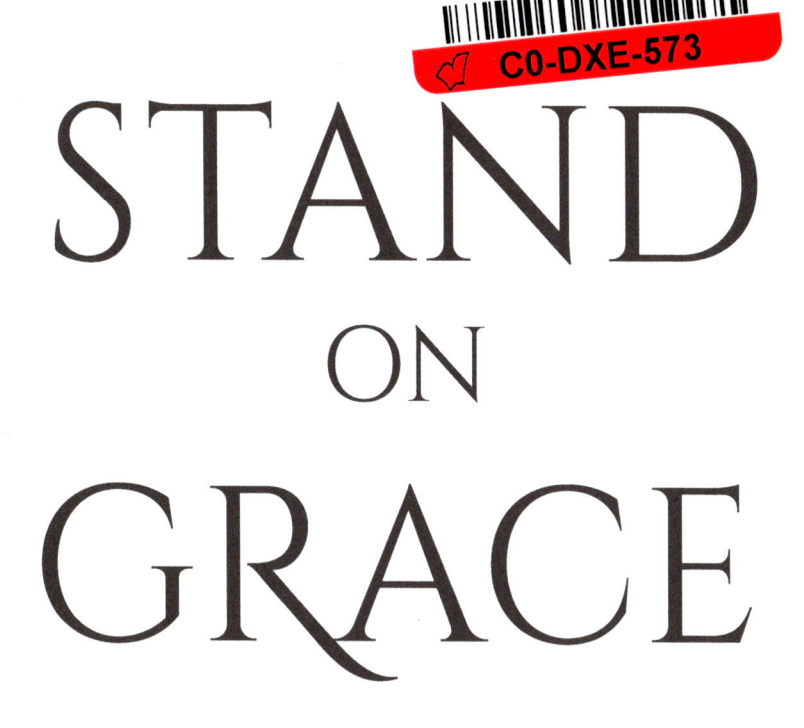

28 Days
Of Biblical
Meditation

STAND ON GRACE

28 Days Of Biblical Meditation

Ava R. Williams

YWNL PUBLISHING
DETROIT

STAND ON GRACE: 28 Days of Biblical Meditation
© 2016 by Ava R. Williams.

All rights reserved. Printed in the United States of America. No part of this book may be used or reproduced in any manner whatsoever without written permission except in the case of brief quotations embodied in critical articles or reviews.

Scripture quotations are taken from the Holy Bible utilizing the New International, English Standard, King James and International Standard Versions. Exact reference to the respective versions has been omitted in order to maintain emphasis on God's unchanging Word as opposed to slight variations in translation or grammatical nuances.

Published in the United States
by YWNL Publishing
Detroit, Michigan

ISBN: 978-0692714119

Library of Congress Control Number: 2016907962

*Don't you know that you yourselves
are God's temple and that God's
Spirit dwells in you?*
~1 Corinthians 3:16

Dedicated to my parents, Gloria McBride-Williams (1956-2010) and Clifton Williams, whose dedication, love and support continue to serve as wonderful earthly examples that have helped me to better understand God's grace, mercy and unconditional love.

Dedicated to all of my family and friends whose support and encouragement have helped me to know God in an even more intimate and profound way.

Dedicated to YOU dear reader. I pray that this book in some way empowers you in your understanding of our heavenly father and helps lead you to victory in all your journeys.

Has God's grace transformed you? Do you have a personal experience or example to share regarding how one of the topics covered in STAND ON GRACE: 28 Days of Biblical Meditation has impacted or been expressed in your life? If so, we'd love to hear from you! Share your story at:

AlwaysStandOnGrace@gmail.com

Contents

Introduction	11
Explanation	17
Instructions	23
FAQ's	27
Week 1: Name It. Overcome It.	35
Day 1: Fear	37
Day 2: Anger	41
Day 3: Hurt	45
Day 4: Doubt	49
Day 5: Guilt	55
Day 6: Stress	59
Day 7: Procrastination	63
Week 2: God of Glory	69
Day 8: God's Identity	71
Day 9: God's Power	75
Day 10: God, the Provider	81
Day 11: God's Faithfulness	87
Day12: God's Grace	91
Day 13: God's Will	97
Day 14: God's Love	103

WEEK 3: Because He Is, We Are.	109
Day 15: Blessings	111
Day 16 :Confidence	117
Day 17: Determination	123
Day 18: Courage	129
Day 19: Integrity	135
Day 20: Healing	141
Day 21: Faith	147
WEEK 4: Great Power, Great Responsibility.	153
Day 22: Gentleness	155
Day 23: Generosity	161
Day 24: Forgiveness	167
Day 25: Tolerance	173
Day 26: Unity	179
Day: 27: Evangelism	185
Day: 28 Love	191
Conclusion	197
About the Author	201

BIBLICAL MEDITATION
Introduction

In a world filled with rhetoric, political biases, competing interests, increasing intolerance and even apathy toward the shocking and ever increasing crises worldwide, it is common to lose faith not only in the world but also in ourselves. It is, especially common, to lose faith in our ability as individuals to affect change. Who do we believe in? Where do we begin? Can we truly make a difference? Is it already too late?

These are questions that I asked myself, and given the world's current state, began to ask myself with increasing frequency. I did not, however, find the answers in my academic or professional development as expected. Although noteworthy, and even impressive, by many standards, these contributed to an even greater sense of despair.

Instead, I had to return to the memories of my youth. I had to reflect upon the brave people that I had read about from a very young age, whose efforts and ideas overturned political regimes, redefined the status quo and reaffirmed the goodness in all of humanity.

These were people such as humanitarian, activist and Civil Rights leader Martin Luther King; Religious Sister and missionary Mother Theresa; the Saint and heroine of France, Joan of Arc; German Student and activist, Sophie Scholl; and young South African revolutionary, Hector Pieterson. They, like a myriad of great historical figures and everyday people, had rallied against, and inspired others to find the courage to rally against, societal ills such as violence, political oppression, racism and many other forms of injustice. Their actions left an indelible mark upon history.

What was it that made them so extraordinary? What was that "thing" that they had in common that gave them the courage to follow their convictions despite the dire repercussions of doing so?

I looked into their academic and professional backgrounds for some clue. Those, however, couldn't have been more diverse. They ranged from peasants with little formal education to college students and pastors.

I looked at their ages surmising that perhaps the wisdom and maturity that comes with age might offer some explanation. Yet, there too, was the discrepancy great with one of these heroes being as young as 13.

I wondered if culture might play a role, if the traditions and customs that defined their heritage might be a factor. Yet, these extraordinary persons lived centuries and continents apart. They lived during the reign of kings, the attempted global domination of oppressive regimes, the struggle for Civil Rights and their fights spanned the battlefields of France, the schoolyards of South Africa, the streets of the USA and beyond.

Whatever it was that they shared in common, it was much more profound than could be explained by cultural, age-related or socio-economic factors.

Delving deeper, looking beyond those things that could be easily measured, the answer become apparent. It was faith.

It was faith.

Many of the extraordinary world changers about whom I had read and come to admire possessed an incredible sense of faith. Somewhere within them was a belief that allowed them to, despite the dire repercussions, look into and beyond themselves in order to see the needs of and fight for the rights of others.

In so doing, in their courage and selflessness, they attained an existence that embodied the very essence of grace.

Grace is a gift that God has bestowed upon us. It is not one that we deserve or are able to earn in any way. Rather, it is a precious gift that God gives us as a result of His unconditional love for us. "For it is by grace you have been saved, through faith--and this not from yourselves, it is the gift of God--not by works, so that no one can boast" (Ephesians 2:8-9).

Through grace God uses us as vessels, working fully within us to reveal Himself not only to us but also to others. Grace is God's divinity within us that: gives us the courage and strength to continue on through great trials; gives us knowledge when no answers seem forthcoming; gives us the resolve to act as we are called, and not merely as expected.

Introduction

And just like those extraordinary persons referenced above, whose actions forever changed history, God's grace is in each and every one of us. As a result, we are extraordinary.

You and I, all of us, are extraordinary!

When we act in accordance with who God calls us to be, we are able to have a true spiritual experience with God. Our existence becomes meaningful. We are able to lead more authentic lives in our homes, communities and world.

STAND ON GRACE: 28 Days of Biblical Meditation seeks to help us discover that voice that resides within each of us that is connected to, and an extension, of God.

STAND ON GRACE combines biblical reflection with principles of meditation to help us to better hear and understand what God desires of, and for us. With such knowledge we will be better equipped to respond when situations, from the simplest to most complex, arise in accordance with God's will for us.

In contrast to the scandals, fallen leaders and prevalence of questionable ideologies and practices, STAND ON GRACE is based upon principles in which we can absolutely believe and trust. It is based upon God's unchanging Word and His never-ending love for all of us.

And it is upon all that God is and the extraordinary and powerful beings that God calls us to be that we can stand.

We can STAND ON GRACE.

BIBLICAL MEDITATION
Explanation

"Let the word of Christ dwell in you richly in all wisdom"
~Colossians 3:16

The Bible encourages us to meditate. In Psalms we see three main principles; prayer, meditation and tribulation. Consider the following:

> But his delight is in the law of the LORD, And in His law he meditates day and night (Psalm 1:2).

> Tremble, and do not sin; Meditate in your heart upon your bed, and be still (Psalm 4:4).

> When I remember Thee on my bed, I meditate on Thee in the night watches (Psalm 63:6).

> I remember the days of old; I meditate on all Thy doings; I muse on the work of Thy hands (Psalm 143:5).

In fact, not only does the Bible encourage us to meditate, it promises good success and a prosperous way to those who do so. In Joshua 1:8 God instructs Joshua "Keep this Book of the Law always on your lips; meditate on it day and night, so that you may be careful to do everything written in it. Then you will be prosperous and successful."

Indeed, King David and Paul were also proponents and practitioners of meditation. Throughout Psalms David declares that he regularly meditates on God, God's ways and God's works. King David affirms "...may my meditation be pleasing to Him, for I rejoice in the LORD" (Psalms 104:34). In Timothy 4:15 the Apostle Paul issues the following instructions "... meditate upon these things; give yourself wholly to them; that your progress may appear to all".

Noteworthy historical church figures such as St. Teresa of Avila and Martin Luther also advocated meditation. In her book, *The Way Of Perfection*, St. Teresa noted "We need no wings to go in search of God, but have only to find a place where we can be alone and look upon Him present within us." Martin Luther provided the faithful with details regarding how to meditate

> "You should meditate not only in your heart, but also externally, by actually repeating and comparing oral

> speech and literal words of the book, reading and rereading them with diligent attention and reflection, so you may see what the Holy Spirit means by them."

Thus, we see that throughout history Christians have practiced meditation and used it as a form of worship and way of connecting more intimately and in a more profound manner with God.

However, the growing emphasis on meditation in eastern religions has caused many to confuse the biblical meditation practiced by Christians with the transcendental meditation associated with Eastern forms of meditation and new Age thinking. This has caused many Christians to become skeptical of, and turn away from, the practice of biblical meditation.

Transcendental meditation, which has become increasingly popular, is NOT biblical meditation.

The two are vastly different.

The stated goal of Eastern meditation is to promote psychological and emotional well-being. This often involves transcendental forms of meditation that revolve around attempts to empty the mind. Often chanting or the repetition of a mantra is involved. Bodily control, such as that over one's own brain waves is emphasized. Emphasis is also placed on becoming detached from the world. This detachment occurs through a process of shedding one's person-hood to escape the confines of what is considered a miserable and limited existence. The purpose is to merge with cosmic forces at work in the universe. Detachment is the final goal. However, as these cosmic forces are often undefined, doing so can render people vulnerable to attacks from malevolent forces.

In contrast, biblical meditation involves filling the mind with what is right and true according to God's Word. It involves the process of reflective thinking via reading and observing portions of Scripture. As we do this God is able to communicate with us through His Word. In so doing, we shed the controlling and hindering influences of the world and become more firmly attached to the living God through Christ.

Scripture, itself, illustrates the purpose and objectives of biblical meditation.

Biblical meditation is a form of worship. It is designed to allow us to commune more intimately with God, by focusing more profoundly on who He is and the wonder of His works. In Psalm 77:11-13 we see, "I shall remember the deeds of the LORD; Surely I will remember Your wonders of old. I will meditate on all Your work And muse on Your deeds. Your way, O God, is holy; What god is great like our God?"

Biblical meditation provides communication with God and instruction for our daily lives. In biblical meditation we communicate with God via the thoughts that come to mind as we reflect upon scripture. This grants us a better understanding of God's Word and how it applies to our lives. In Psalms 119: 27; 97 we see "Help me understand how your precepts function, and I will meditate on your wondrous acts... How I love your instruction! Every day it is my meditation."

Biblical meditation motivates and encourages us. It inspires us and provides us with the strength and courage to fulfill God's plans for us.

> "Do not be afraid, you who are highly esteemed," he said. "Peace! Be strong now; be strong." When he spoke to me, I was strengthened and said, "Speak, my Lord, since you have given me strength" (Daniel 10:19).

> This Book of the Law shall not depart from your mouth, but you shall meditate on it day and night, so that you may be careful to do according to all that is written in it. For then you will make your way prosperous, and then you will have good success (Joshua 1:8).

Biblical meditation leads to a renewed mind. It allows God to perfect us and change the way we think. It helps us to think and act in accordance with the Word and will of God.

> Do not conform to the pattern of this world, but be transformed by the renewing of your mind. Then you will be able to test and approve what God's will is--his good, pleasing and perfect will (Romans 12:2).

> I have more insight than all my teachers, for I meditate on your statutes (Psalm 119:99).

Biblical meditation is more than just a practice. It is an act of faith. It serves as evidence of our desire for God's presence in our lives. It allows us to better understand God and His plan for us. It empowers us to resist the negative pressures and temptations of the world. Perhaps most beautifully, it allows us to actively express our gratitude for the grace, redemption, forgiveness and love that God bestows upon us.

BIBLICAL MEDITATION
Instructions

Biblical meditation is not overly complicated. It can be accomplished in as little as 10 minutes per day. Remember, God desires an intimate relationship with us! He wants us to know and love Him. He does not make this task difficult. "And you shall love the LORD your God with all your heart, with all your soul, with all your mind, and with all your strength; This is the first commandment" (Mark 12:30).

1 Timothy 2:4 reminds us that God "... desires all men to be saved and to come to the knowledge of the truth." Such is the desire of God that as John 16:13 reminds us "God has given us the Spirit of Truth that will guide us into all truth."

The following steps will guide you in your biblical meditations of worship and fellowship with God.

Begin by quieting your thoughts in order to attach yourself more firmly to God. This means stilling preoccupations with the day's worries, temporarily putting aside your thoughts about an ailing relative, caregiver situation and professional responsibilities. This even means temporarily ignoring text messages and Facebook status updates in order to truly prepare yourself to enter into a state of spiritual oneness with God. This must be done so that you are truly able to reflect upon and absorb the Scriptures that you are about to read. Techniques such as the use of worship music, a personalized opening prayer of invitation to God, or focusing on your breathing may be utilized to aid you in this process. As you proceed through the guided biblical meditations you may wish to combine or vary your techniques. The suggested time for this is 2-5 minutes.

Read and reflect upon the biblical meditations. As you read the provided text, truly think about God's Word in your mind. This should be a time of reflection, reverence and worship. Ask God to assist you through the Holy Spirit in understanding the scriptures. Suggested time is 5-15 minutes

Close the biblical meditation section by reflecting even more deeply upon how the topic pertains to your life or current circumstances. Focus on what action(s) God may be requiring of you and seek solutions in accordance with what God is calling you to do. Suggested prayers are provided to aid in this process. Suggested time is 3-15 minutes.

If desired, read the section containing additional biblical references pertaining to the selected topic. The additional biblical references section is optional.

Remember that while these reflections may be brief, they are also designed to give us insight into God's plan for our lives. Once we have received this knowledge it is important to implement it.

> Do not merely listen to the word, and so deceive yourselves. Do what it says. Anyone who listens to the word but does not do what it says is like a man who looks at his face in a mirror and, after looking at himself, goes away and immediately forgets what he looks like. But the man who looks intently into the perfect law that gives freedom, and continues to do this, not forgetting what he has heard, but doing it--he will be blessed in what he does (James 1:22-25).

BIBLICAL MEDITATION *FAQ's*

What is the right time to meditate?

Every person is different and so the answer to this question varies. Some people may find it helpful to do their biblical meditations first thing in the morning. Often, the waking hours before life has a chance to fully intrude serve as a perfect moment to enter into communion with God. As an old adage goes "You have time for the first thing that you do every morning." Biblical meditation is a wonderful way to start. Practicing it first thing in the morning ensures that it is done.

For others, some point during the day may prove best. Biblical meditation offers us respite from the woes and demands of the world. People who, for example, work in extremely stressful or unpleasant atmospheres or happen to be in the midst of a very trying situation, will find it beneficial to hit "the stop button" and consciously gain control of and invite God into their situation.

For some people, however, evening, especially the time just before bed may be ideal. It has been said that the last thing you focus your mind on before going to sleep will remain in your subconscious throughout the night. Prominent biblical figures such as Joshua and King David meditated at night.

It is helpful, however, to select a set time during the day that you will meditate and adhere to as much as possible. This will help establish biblical meditation as a regular practice in your life.

No matter what time you select, biblical meditation is a moment of spiritual oneness with God. When we open our thoughts to God, those thoughts will consciously or subconsciously influence our attitudes and actions throughout that day or the next.

If God knows my every thought why do I need to meditate?

God does not violate the free will that he has granted us. When we need God to take action in our lives, we must invite Him to do so. Biblical meditation expresses our desire for God to act in our lives. It positions us to receive all the blessings that he wishes to bestow upon us.

What are the benefits of biblical meditation?

Biblical meditation involves pro-actively setting aside time to enter into worship and fellowship with God. It is a time for us to communicate directly and intimately with God. To do so requires an investment of time, inner quiet and conscientiously opening our hearts and ourselves to God. Biblical meditation teaches us to shut out intrusions and negative stimuli. This results in the development of a quiet spirit. Jesus possessed inner calm. Biblical meditation empowers us in our search to become more like Christ. Biblical meditation increases our appreciation for, understanding of and sensitivity to God.

As a result, it is often a time during which God provides us with, or prepares us to begin receiving, instruction. When we meditate on God's Word and are able to be truly obedient we open ourselves to receive a multitude of blessings. As noted in the Bible, this includes; success and prosperity (Joshua 1:8), fruitfulness (Psalms1:1-3), wisdom and insight (Psalms 119:98-99), joy (Psalms 63:6), and victory over sin (Psalms 119:11).

What if I don't receive an answer?

You may not receive immediate clarity on a specific topic. You may need to repeat certain passages or topics several times. This is a time for you to communicate directly and intimately with God. Ask Him to provide you with greater clarity. As He reveals these insights and instruction ask Him how to apply that truth to your life.

If God seems silent, perhaps he is still preparing you for His answer and you need more time to hear and obey His will. He may still be preparing your circumstances. Also consider whether or not you are truly being obedient to God's will. Perhaps sin is still controlling an area of your life. In these instances God may need more time with you in order to prepare you to receive His blessings.

Remember that God's wisdom and timing are not our own. God may have already answered your question. The answer may even exceed what you originally sought. Sometimes we must continue praying and meditating until we see that God has already answered us.

How long do I need to meditate?

This will vary according to each individual. As

previously noted, the Bible encourages us to meditate often.

> This Book of the Law shall not depart from your mouth, but you shall meditate on it day and night, so that you may be careful to do according to all that is written in it. For then you will make your way prosperous, and then you will have good success (Joshua 1:8).

The biblical meditations in STAND ON GRACE have been designed for you to complete them in as little as 10 minutes. They are designed to promote fellowship, worship and dialogue that extends far beyond the time spent meditating.

In general it requires about 18-66 days for a particular practice to become a habit. STAND ON GRACE provides 28 days of guided biblical meditation. STAND ON GRACE is designed to aid in firmly setting you on a journey that will help you turn this wonderful and blessed practice into a lifelong habit.

What if I miss a day or two?

Do not be discouraged if you miss a day or two. Just remember all the wonderful benefits associated with biblical meditation. Identify the factors that may have hindered your progress so that you can prevent them from continuing to do so. Most importantly, forgive yourself and continue.

The biblical meditations in STAND ON GRACE are progressively structured. If you miss a day or a few, you may want to reread a few passages before proceeding to the next topic. You may also pick up from where you left off.

Day 1: Fear	37
Day 2: Anger	41
Day 3: Hurt	45
Day 4: Doubt	49
Day 5: Guilt	55
Day 6: Stress	59
Day 7: Procrastination	63

Week 1

BIBLICAL MEDITATION TOPIC
Name It. Overcome It.

God has given us dominion and authority over all earthly woes and conditions. These include illness and negative emotions such as fear, doubt and worry among many others. In order to understand the authority, which God instills within us, we must first understand the nature of such occurrences and how God calls us to respond to them.

TOPIC
Fear

"For I am the LORD, your God, who takes hold of your right hand and says to you, Do not fear; I will help you."
~Isaiah 41:13

OPENING MEDITATION: 2 - 5 MINUTES
BIBLICAL MEDITATION: 5 - 15 MINUTES
CLOSING MEDITATION: 3 - 10 MINUTES

Quick Reference Guide: Biblical Meditation Instructions

Begin the opening meditation by quieting your thoughts in order to attach yourself more firmly to God.

Read the biblical meditations. Reflect upon how the topic pertains to your life or current circumstances.

Close the biblical meditations by focusing on what action(s) God may be requiring of you. Seek solutions in accordance with what God is calling you to do. Suggested prayers are provided to aid in this process.

If desired, read the section containing additional biblical references pertaining to the selected topic.

Day 1: Fear

Fear may arise within us unexpectedly. It may range from a slight sensation of discomfort or unease to a paralyzing feeling of dread. It may be a temporary sensation caused by something we find unpleasant such as a spider or by sudden or impending change. In order to understand the ramifications of fear in our life it is important to understand what the Bible says about fear.

The Bible speaks of two types of fear: fear of the Lord and the spirit of fear. Fear of the Lord is regarded as positive and praiseworthy. It is best understood as a form of reverence and respect. For example:

> My son, if you receive my words and treasure up my commandments with you, making your ear attentive to wisdom and inclining your heart to understanding; yes, if you call out for insight and raise your voice for understanding, if you seek it like silver and search for it as for hidden treasures, then you will understand the fear of the LORD and find the knowledge of God. For the LORD gives wisdom; from his mouth comes knowledge and understanding… (Proverbs 2:1-6).

In contrast, the spirit of fear is not of God and causes us to experience negative emotions and even react in ways that are harmful to our well-being and that undermine our faith. We are reminded:

> Have I not commanded you? Be strong and courageous. Do not be frightened, and do not be dismayed, for the Lord your God is with you wherever you go (Joshua 1:9).

Suggested Prayer:

God, help me to identify and release my fears. Help me to seek you more boldly and more courageously so that I may better understand and implement what you desire of, and for me, in my life.

Additional Biblical References:

> **Proverbs 14:27** The fear of the Lord is a fountain of life, that one may turn away from the snares of death.

> **Job 3:25** For the thing that I fear comes upon me, and what I dread befalls me.

> **Psalm 27:1-3** Of David. The Lord is my light and my salvation; whom shall I fear? The Lord is the stronghold of my life; of whom shall I be afraid? When evildoers assail me to eat up my flesh, my adversaries and foes, it is they who stumble and fall. Though an army encamp against me, my heart shall not fear; though war arise against me, yet I will be confident.

Day 2

BIBLICAL MEDITATION TOPIC

Anger

"Better a patient man than a warrior, a man who controls his temper than one who takes a city."
~Proverbs 16:32

OPENING MEDITATION: 2 - 5 MINUTES
BIBLICAL MEDITATION: 5 - 15 MINUTES
CLOSING MEDITATION: 3 - 10 MINUTES

Quick Reference Guide: Biblical Meditation Instructions

Begin the opening meditation by quieting your thoughts in order to attach yourself more firmly to God.

Read the biblical meditations. Reflect upon how the topic pertains to your life or current circumstances.

Close the biblical meditations by focusing on what action(s) God may be requiring of you. Seek solutions in accordance with what God is calling you to do. Suggested prayers are provided to aid in this process.

If desired, read the section containing additional biblical references pertaining to the selected topic.

Day 2: Anger

Anger is one of the most intense and potentially most destructive emotions that we can experience as human beings. It can be triggered by a slight offense or caused by long standing issues and frustrations. Whatever the cause, when left unaddressed anger can have a negative impact on our emotional well-being, lead to illness and cause irreparable damage to relationships.

The significance of anger in the Bible is twofold. In one sense, anger is likened to righteousness. Righteous anger is indignation prompted by sinful actions such as injustice being forced upon others. For example:

> For the wrath of God is revealed from heaven against all ungodliness and unrighteousness of men, who by their unrighteousness suppress the truth (Romans 1:18).

In another context, anger itself becomes a sin. This occurs when we fail to control our anger and allow it to breed malice, wrath, dissension and sinful practices. Such things threaten our relationship with God and allow Satan to use us.

> ...but for Cain and his offering he [the LORD] had no regard. So Cain was very angry, and his face fell. The LORD said to Cain, "Why are you angry, and why has your face fallen? If you do well, will you not be accepted? And if you do not do well, sin is crouching at the door.

Its desire is for you, but you must rule over it." Cain spoke to Abel his brother. And when they were in the field, Cain rose up against his brother Abel and killed him" (Genesis 4:5-8).

Suggested Prayer:

God, help me to identify the source(s) of my anger, how it manifests itself in my life as well as how it affects those around me. God, help me to use indignation and outrage that results from injustices in a manner that affirms your glory in my life and the life of others.

Additional Biblical References:

Proverbs 20:22 Do not say, "I'll pay you back for this wrong!" Wait for the LORD, and He will deliver you.

Ephesians 4:26-7 "In your anger do not sin: Do not let the sun go down while you are still angry, and do not give the devil a foothold."

Matthew 5:21-24 You have heard that it was said to the people long ago, "Do not murder, and anyone who murders will be subject to judgment." But I tell you that anyone who is angry with his brother will be subject to judgment …first go and be reconciled to your brother; then come and offer your gift.

Day 3

BIBLICAL MEDITATION TOPIC
Hurt

"Cast your burden on the LORD and He will sustain you."
~Psalm 55:22

OPENING MEDITATION: 2 - 5 MINUTES
BIBLICAL MEDITATION: 5 - 15 MINUTES
CLOSING MEDITATION: 3 - 10 MINUTES

QUICK REFERENCE GUIDE: BIBLICAL MEDITATION INSTRUCTIONS

Begin the opening meditation by quieting your thoughts in order to attach yourself more firmly to God.

Read the biblical meditations. Reflect upon how the topic pertains to your life or current circumstances.

Close the biblical meditations by focusing on what action(s) God may be requiring of you. Seek solutions in accordance with what God is calling you to do. Suggested prayers are provided to aid in this process.

If desired, read the section containing additional biblical references pertaining to the selected topic.

Day 3: Hurt

Hurt is a nearly inevitable part of the human existence. At some point we will all find ourselves on the receiving end of some intentional or non-deliberate offence. Such occurrences may cause great distress and sadness.

From Jeremiah, to Paul to Jesus, there are ample examples of people experiencing hurt throughout the Bible.

> The tears stream from my eyes, an artesian well of tears, until You, God, look down from on high. You look and see my tears. You listened when I called out, 'Don't shut your ears! Get me out of here! Save me! You came close when I called out. You said, 'It's going to be all right.' "You took my side, Master – You brought me back to life" (Lamentations 3:49-51)!

The manner in which we respond to hurt becomes a measure of our faith. We are to take our hurt to God and seek comfort and solace in Him. Additionally, we are called to not further perpetuate our hurt. Explaining how Jesus dealt with hurt and personal offence, 1 Peter 2:23 writes "When He was reviled, He did not revile in return; when He suffered He did not threaten; but He trusted to Him Who judges justly."

Suggested Prayer:

God, help me to release all hurt both hidden and known from within my heart. Let me look first and always to you for comfort and solace. Let me respond to hurt only in ways that reflect your glory.

Additional Biblical References:

Psalm 50:15 Call upon Me in the day of trouble.

Romans 12:17-19 Repay no one evil for evil, but take thought for what is noble in the sight of all... Beloved, never avenge yourselves but leave it to the wrath of God, for it is written "Vengeance is mine, I will repay," says the Lord.

Matthew 11:28-30 Come unto me, all [ye] that labour and are heavy laden, and I will give you rest.

DAY 4

BIBLICAL MEDITATION TOPIC

Doubt

"He who doubts is like a wave of the sea, blown and tossed by the wind."
~James 1:6

OPENING MEDITATION: 2 - 5 MINUTES
BIBLICAL MEDITATION: 5 - 15 MINUTES
CLOSING MEDITATION: 3 - 10 MINUTES

Quick Reference Guide: Biblical Meditation Instructions

Begin the opening meditation by quieting your thoughts in order to attach yourself more firmly to God.

Read the biblical meditations. Reflect upon how the topic pertains to your life or current circumstances.

Close the biblical meditations by focusing on what action(s) God may be requiring of you. Seek solutions in accordance with what God is calling you to do. Suggested prayers are provided to aid in this process.

If desired, read the section containing additional biblical references pertaining to the selected topic.

Day 4: Doubt

Doubt occurs when we allow human reasoning and human logic to overshadow our faith in God. The Bible shows us that it was in the Garden of Eden when the serpent tempted Eve that doubt was first introduced in the heart of man.

> Now the serpent was more crafty than any other beast of the field that the Lord God had made. He said to the woman, "Did God actually say, 'You shall not eat of any tree in the garden?" And the woman said to the serpent, "We may eat of the fruit of the trees in the garden, but God said, 'You shall not eat of the fruit of the tree that is in the midst of the garden, neither shall you touch it, lest you die.' But the serpent said to the woman, "You will not surely die" (Genesis 3 1-4).

Doubt gives the enemy power over us, undermines our confidence in God's Word, questions God's judgment and threatens God's plans for our lives.

In the Bible we are prompted to remember the deeds of the Lord and remember the miracles of long ago.

> I shall remember the deeds of the LORD; Surely I will remember Your wonders of old. I will meditate on all Your work And muse on Your deeds. Your way, O God, is holy; "What god is great like our God?" (Psalm 77:10-13).

When we dutifully do this, we can avoid instances of consternation and doubt such as when Thomas demanded to see the risen Jesus before he believed in the resurrection. Or when Zechariah doubted that he and his wife would conceive a child as God had promised, because he believed himself to old to do so.

> "He delivers and rescues and performs signs and wonders In heaven and on earth, Who has also delivered Daniel from the power of the lions." So this Daniel enjoyed success in the reign of Darius and in the reign of Cyrus the Persian (Daniel 6:27-28).

We must not doubt God's presence in our lives nor God's plans for us. We must remember that God equips us to do all that he has called us to do. Often God's plans for us are so grandiose that they exceed anything we have ever experienced or are able to explain using the world's logic.

Suggested Prayer:

God, empower me to act out of faith rather than doubt. Equip me to boldly ascend to the heights that you, and you alone, define. Strengthen me when my faith is tested and remove any feelings or beliefs that are not in agreement with your will for me.

Additional Biblical References:

Matthew 14:31 Jesus immediately reached out his hand and took hold of him, saying to him, "O you of little faith, why did you doubt?"

Psalm 77:11 I will remember the deeds of the LORD; yes, I will remember your miracles of long ago.

Mark 11:23 Truly, I say to you, whoever says to this mountain, 'Be taken up and thrown into the sea,' and does not doubt in his heart, but believes that what he says will come to pass, it will be done for him.

DAY 5

BIBLICAL MEDITATION TOPIC

Guilt

"If we confess our sins, he is faithful and just to forgive us our sins and to cleanse us from all unrighteousness."
~1 John 1:9

OPENING MEDITATION: 2 - 5 MINUTES
BIBLICAL MEDITATION: 5 - 15 MINUTES
CLOSING MEDITATION: 3 - 10 MINUTES

Quick Reference Guide: Biblical Meditation Instructions

Begin the opening meditation by quieting your thoughts in order to attach yourself more firmly to God.

Read the biblical meditations. Reflect upon how the topic pertains to your life or current circumstances.

Close the biblical meditations by focusing on what action(s) God may be requiring of you. Seek solutions in accordance with what God is calling you to do. Suggested prayers are provided to aid in this process.

If desired, read the section containing additional biblical references pertaining to the selected topic.

Day 5: Guilt

Guilt becomes destructive when we allow our conscience to become enslaved by past actions, imperfections or sins. The enemy uses our feelings of guilt to torment us and convince us that we are horrible, worthless, unlovable and damaged beyond repair.

The Bible addresses this issue, and in it, we find that guilt has a dual significance. Guilt that results in genuine repentance comes from the Holy Spirit and frees, heals and strengthens our relationship with God. This is often referred to as conviction and/or Godly sorrow. For example:

> Godly sorrow brings repentance that leads to salvation and leaves no regret, but worldly sorrow brings death (2 Corinthians 7:10).

The Bible also speaks of another form of guilt that is destructive and perpetuates the lie that our actions are unforgivable. It robs us of joy and undermines our confidence and faith. This is known as condemnation. It is the most powerful weapon that the enemy uses against us.

We must counter such attacks by truly understanding that in all things God forgives us, wipes the slate completely clean and desires to have a pure and profound relationship with us. So great is this desire that out of love for us, God gave His only son.

> "How much more shall the blood of Christ, who through the eternal spirit offered himself without spot to God, purge your conscience from dead works to serve the living God?" (Hebrews 9:14).

Suggested Prayer:

God, please free me from all feelings of guilt. Strengthen me so that the enemy is not able to exploit my weakness and I may genuinely stand before you with a pure heart and renewed spirit.

Additional Biblical References:

Micah 7:19 You will again have compassion on us; you will tread our sins underfoot and hurl all our iniquities into the depth of the sea.

2 Corinthians 5:17 "Therefore if any man be in Christ, he is a new creature: old things are passed away; behold, all things are become new."

Isaiah 43:25 I, even I, am he who blots out your transgressions, for my own sake, and remembers your sins no more

DAY 6

BIBLICAL MEDITATION TOPIC
Stress

"Trust in the LORD with all your heart, and do not lean on your own understanding. In all your ways acknowledge him, and he will make straight your paths."
~Proverbs 3:5-6

OPENING MEDITATION: 2 - 5 MINUTES
BIBLICAL MEDITATION: 5 - 15 MINUTES
CLOSING MEDITATION: 3 - 10 MINUTES

Quick Reference Guide: Biblical Meditation Instructions

Begin the opening meditation by quieting your thoughts in order to attach yourself more firmly to God.

Read the biblical meditations. Reflect upon how the topic pertains to your life or current circumstances.

Close the biblical meditations by focusing on what action(s) God may be requiring of you. Seek solutions in accordance with what God is calling you to do. Suggested prayers are provided to aid in this process.

If desired, read the section containing additional biblical references pertaining to the selected topic.

Day 6: Stress

Stress can be caused by, and result in, a myriad of negative emotions such as anxiety, worry, doubt and fear. It can be caused, for example, by a perceived lack of resources among many other factors.

Worldly understanding defines the acquisition of more and more material resources as the solution to stress and its results in our lives.

The Bible, however, offers an alternative explanation of stress.

While stress may be a commonplace in our lives, the Bible does not define it as a normal occurrence. The Bible, in fact, defines stress as an anomaly. Furthermore, when left unchecked stress can rule our lives and even cause us to shut down completely.

> "Therefore I tell you, do not be anxious about your life, what you will eat or what you will drink, nor about your body, what you will put on. Is not life more than food and the body more than clothing? And which of you by being anxious can add a single hour to his span of life" (Matthew 6:25, 27)?

Materialism and money are not the answer to stress and can exacerbate our feelings of unease as we struggle to accumulate something of which there will seemingly never be enough. The solution resides in learning to truly trust in God and turning all our concerns and burdens over to Him. When we realize that we are never alone and that we have a God who sustains and will never fail us we regain our power over stressful situations.

> "Do not be anxious about anything, but in everything by prayer and supplication with thanksgiving let your requests be made known to God. And the peace of God, which surpasses all understanding, will guard your hearts and your minds in Christ Jesus" (Philippians 4:6-7).

Suggested Prayer:

God, help me to fill my heart and my mind with your Word. When situations and circumstances arise that threaten the peace that you intend for me, help me to lean not on my own understanding but on absolute trust and faith in You.

Additional Biblical References:

> **Psalm 55:22** Cast your burden on the Lord, and he will sustain you; he will never permit the righteous to be moved.

> **1 Peter 4:12** "Beloved, do not be surprised at the fiery trial when it comes upon you to test you, as though something strange were happening to you."

> **Psalm 34:4** "I sought the LORD, and he answered me and delivered me from all my fears."

Day 7

BIBLICAL MEDITATION TOPIC
Procrastination

"You need to persevere so that when you have done the will of God, you will receive what he has promised."
~Hebrews 10:36

OPENING MEDITATION: 2 - 5 MINUTES
BIBLICAL MEDITATION: 5 - 15 MINUTES
CLOSING MEDITATION: 3 - 10 MINUTES

Quick Reference Guide: Biblical Meditation Instructions

Begin the opening meditation by quieting your thoughts in order to attach yourself more firmly to God.

Read the biblical meditations. Reflect upon how the topic pertains to your life or current circumstances.

Close the biblical meditations by focusing on what action(s) God may be requiring of you. Seek solutions in accordance with what God is calling you to do. Suggested prayers are provided to aid in this process.

If desired, read the section containing additional biblical references pertaining to the selected topic.

Day 7: Procrastination

Procrastination adds needless stress and anxiety to our lives. Often, it steals our joy and hinders our ability to receive God's blessings and many ways in which he wishes to prosper us. Procrastination, when left unaddressed, can derail God's plans for our lives.

While the actual word procrastination does not appear in the Bible, the theme, its causes and its consequences appear frequently.

Indecision can lead to procrastination. The Bible notes "A double minded man is unstable in all he does" (James 1:8).

Perfectionism can also result in procrastination. Negative self-talk and unrealistic expectations can become paralyzing. Ecclesiastes 11:4 cautions us "If you wait for perfect conditions, you'll never get anything done!"

Negative emotions such as fear, doubt and guilt are traps. They cause us to question our own abilities or mercilessly berate ourselves when unforeseen situations or circumstances arise.

When obstacles occur that make it impossible for us to complete a task in an intended manner or time frame, we are to keep moving forward. We are to keep persevering. In Hebrews 10:35 we are reminded "So don't lose your confidence, since it holds a great reward for you."

We are commanded to be diligent in our work, regardless of the task, remembering that ultimately whatever we do we should be doing it to please the Lord "Whatever you do, work at it with all your heart, as working for the Lord, not for men" (Colossians 3:23).

We are also cautioned that there are situations in which we absolutely must not procrastinate. One of which is when it comes to reconciling with someone we have offended. In Ephesians 4:26 "Do not let the sun go down while you are still angry." To do so, is to give the enemy power and point of entry in our lives.

Most importantly, Christians are commanded not to procrastinate strengthening their spiritual relationship with God as well as sharing the gospel with those who may be unfamiliar with or are in need of it. In this there is particular urgency. "Yet you do not know what tomorrow will bring what is your life? For you are a mist that appears for a little time..."(James 4:13–14). "Most importantly, you also must be ready, for the Son of Man is coming at an hour you do not expect" (Luke 12:40).

Day 7: Procrastination

Suggested Prayer:

God, help me to understand any doubt, fear, disbelief or anger that may cause me to procrastinate. Remove these from my life, from my spirit, so that I am freed, cleansed and renewed and able to diligently and joyfully do all that you ask of me and receive all that you intend for me.

Additional Biblical References:

> **Jeremiah 29:11** "For I know the plans that I have for you," declares the Lord, "plans for well-being, and not for calamity, in order to give you a future and a hope."

> **Hebrews 3:12–13** Take care, brothers, lest there be in any of you an evil, unbelieving heart, leading you to fall away from the living God. But exhort one another every day, as long as it is called "today" that none of you may be hardened by the deceitfulness of sin.

> **Proverbs 13:4** Lazy people want much but get little, while the diligent are prospering.

Day 8: God's Identity	71
Day 9: God's Power	75
Day 10: God, the Provider	81
Day 11: God's Faithfulness	87
Day 12: God's Grace	91
Day 13: God's Will	97
Day 14: God's Love	103

WEEK 2

BIBLICAL MEDITATION TOPIC
God of Glory

During the first part of our biblical meditation we explored the negative thoughts, actions and emotions that prevent us from fully manifesting the greatness with which God equips us as well as fully receiving the blessings that He wishes to bestow upon us.

In order to truly understand who God calls us, and equips us, to be we must first understand who God is and who we are in Him.

During this second week we focus on God and His presence in our lives.

DAY 8

BIBLICAL MEDITATION TOPIC
God's Identity

"For you, O Lord, are good and forgiving, abounding in steadfast love to all who call upon you."
~Psalms 86:5

OPENING MEDITATION: 2 - 5 MINUTES
BIBLICAL MEDITATION: 5 - 15 MINUTES
CLOSING MEDITATION: 3 - 10 MINUTES

Quick Reference Guide: Biblical Meditation Instructions

Begin the opening meditation by quieting your thoughts in order to attach yourself more firmly to God.

Read the biblical meditations. Reflect upon how the topic pertains to your life or current circumstances.

Close the biblical meditations by focusing on what action(s) God may be requiring of you. Seek solutions in accordance with what God is calling you to do. Suggested prayers are provided to aid in this process.

If desired, read the section containing additional biblical references pertaining to the selected topic.

Day 8: God's Identity

God wants us to know Him! Not as a theory, not as an ideology nor as merely an abstract figure that we read about or listen to others explain. Rather, God desires for us to know and experience Him in a personal, intimate and very real manner. As a result God reveals Himself to us through His acts, through written revelation and through our fellowship with Him.

In the Bible God names everyone and everything. God even names Himself numerous times in the Bible and in so doing gives us the power to call upon Him.

Name	Meaning/Significance
Elohim	Power, Strength and Might
El Shaddai	The Almighty
Adonai	God the Son as Sovereign Master
YHWH or Jehovah	I Am That I Am
Jehovah-Jireh	God the Provider
Jehovah-Rophe	God that Heals
Jehovah-Nissi	God my Banner, my Victor, my Protector
Jehovah-Shalom	God is Peace
Jehovah-Rohi	The Lord my Shepherd
Jehovah-Shammah	The Lord is There
Jehovah-Tsidkenu	The Lord our Righteousness

As seen above, God is known by many names. Each name gives us greater insight into God's identity.

This allows us to better understand who HE is, and as a result, who we are in Him.

Suggested Prayer:

God, help me to know your name not only as it is written and as others may refer to you, but as it is engraved on my heart and in my spirit. Help me to call upon your name not only in moments of trial but also during times of jubilation!

Additional Biblical References:

2 Samuel 22:32-34 For who is God besides the LORD? And who is the Rock except our God? It is God who arms me with strength and makes my way perfect. He makes my feet like the feet of a deer; he enables me to stand on the heights.

Acts 10:34 Then Peter began to speak: "I now realize how true it is that God does not show favoritism."

Revelation 21:3 And I heard a loud voice from the throne saying, "Now the dwelling of God is with men, and he will live with them. They will be his people, and God himself will be with them and be their God."

DAY
9

BIBLICAL MEDITATION TOPIC
God's Power

"Ah Lord GOD! Behold, Thou hast made the heavens and the earth by Thy great power and by Thine outstretched arm! Nothing is too difficult for Thee."
~Jeremiah 32:17

OPENING MEDITATION: 2 - 5 MINUTES
BIBLICAL MEDITATION: 5 - 15 MINUTES
CLOSING MEDITATION: 3 - 10 MINUTES

Quick Reference Guide: Biblical Meditation Instructions

Begin the opening meditation by quieting your thoughts in order to attach yourself more firmly to God.

Read the biblical meditations. Reflect upon how the topic pertains to your life or current circumstances.

Close the biblical meditations by focusing on what action(s) God may be requiring of you. Seek solutions in accordance with what God is calling you to do. Suggested prayers are provided to aid in this process.

If desired, read the section containing additional biblical references pertaining to the selected topic.

Day 9: God's Power

God is omnipotent and able to do all things. He has no earthly nor heavenly limits. Throughout the Bible we see example after example that affirms God's incomparable power. The Bible provides a myriad of examples and definitions of God's power.

The story of creation offers us the first glimpse. "…His eternal power and divine nature, have been clearly seen, being understood through what has been made…" (Romans 1:20). This is followed by amazing feats such freeing the Israelites from enslavement in Egypt, "He sent signs and wonders into your midst, O Egypt, Upon Pharaoh and all his servant" (Psalms 139:9).

The ultimate manifestations of God's power, however, are the life, death and resurrection of Jesus Christ.

Among an infinite number of attributes, we see that God's power: Creates, establishes and governs all things Jeremiah 10:12; Conquers death 1Corinthians 6:14; Delivers believers Psalms 106:8; Destroys the wicked Romans 9:22; and more.

> And what is the immeasurable greatness of his power toward us who believe, according to the working of his great might that he worked in Christ when he raised him from the dead and seated him at his right hand

in the heavenly places, far above all rule and authority and power and dominion, and above every name that is named, not only in this age but also in the one to come (Ephesians 1:19-21).

Because of God's grace, God's power has implications in, and for, our lives. God's power removes all weakness and limits.

God's power perfects us in our weakness "And He has said to me, "My grace is sufficient for you, for power is perfected in weakness" (2 Corinthians 12:9).

God's power saves, sanctifies and empowers us. We are not to depend on, nor even trust, our human strengths and methods. Instead we are to depend completely on God's power, which works on our behalf through grace. When we do so we give glory to God. Truly trusting in God allows us to live a life filled with hope and faith, knowing that if God has called us, then His purpose for us will be fulfilled.

Suggested Prayer:

In recognition and reverence of your immeasurable power, I boldly and unwaveringly declare that you, and you alone are able. I humble myself, God, and pray that you empower me and use me as a vessel to demonstrate your power and do your work.

Additional Biblical References:

1 Chronicles 29:11 Yours, O Lord, is the greatness and the power and the glory and the victory and the majesty, for all that is in the heavens and in the earth is yours. Yours is the kingdom, O Lord, and you are exalted as head above all.

2 Corinthians 12:9-10 "My grace is enough for you, for my power is made perfect in weakness." So then, I will boast most gladly about my weaknesses, so that the power of Christ may reside in me. Therefore I am content with weaknesses, with insults, with troubles, with persecutions and difficulties for the sake of Christ, for whenever I am weak, then I am strong.

Ephesians 1:18-19 Since the eyes of your heart have been enlightened – so that you may know what is the hope of his calling, what is the wealth of his glorious inheritance in the saints, and what is the incomparable greatness of his power toward us who believe, as displayed in the exercise of his immense strength.

DAY
10

BIBLICAL MEDITATION TOPIC

God, the Provider

"But my God shall supply all your needs according to his riches in glory by Christ Jesus."
~Philippians 4:19

OPENING MEDITATION: 2 - 5 MINUTES
BIBLICAL MEDITATION: 5 - 15 MINUTES
CLOSING MEDITATION: 3 - 10 MINUTES

Quick Reference Guide: Biblical Meditation Instructions

Begin the opening meditation by quieting your thoughts in order to attach yourself more firmly to God.

Read the biblical meditations. Reflect upon how the topic pertains to your life or current circumstances.

Close the biblical meditations by focusing on what action(s) God may be requiring of you. Seek solutions in accordance with what God is calling you to do. Suggested prayers are provided to aid in this process.

If desired, read the section containing additional biblical references pertaining to the selected topic.

Day 10: God, the Provider

God is committed to fulfilling our needs. The Bible highlights example after example of God fulfilling the spiritual, emotional and physical needs of the faithful. We are assured that no need is too great for God to meet and that He graciously and generously seeks to provide us with only the best.

> The Lord shall command the blessing upon you in your storehouse and in all that you undertake. And He will bless you in the land which the Lord your God gives you. And the Lord shall make you have surplus of prosperity, through the fruit of your body, of your livestock, and of your ground, in the land which the Lord swore to your fathers to give you. The Lord shall open to you His good treasury, the heavens to give the rain of your land in its season and to bless all the work of your hands; and you shall lend to many nations, but you shall not borrow (Deuteronomy 28:8, 11-12).

And yet, there are times, when it seems as though our needs have gone unmet and our prayers have not been answered. Through scriptural explanation we see that this may occur for one of several reasons:

Confusing needs with wants – God's wisdom far exceeds our own. In contrast to us, He is able, in every situation, to discern between that which we truly need and that which we may really want.

Taking scripture out of context – the promise to supply our needs applies to the faithful, not those who live in rebellion. Often, sins must be treated before prayers can be answered.

Not asking with a pure heart – First, we must ask. Our prayers must also not be motivated by selfishness.

Failing to do our part – we must not be lazy or procrastinate. We must do our part so that God can do His.

Impatience – God's time is not our time. When we seek answers from God we must wait on His response.

Not obeying God's instructions – We must do as God commands us even when it involves the unexpected. God's methods are not our own and the results often surpass anything that we are able to imagine.

Lack of faith in God – During times of hardship we allow our needs to become greater than God, losing focus and shaking our faith. We must remember, even during difficult times, that nothing is beyond God. God fulfills every promise.

We, ourselves, often hinder the answers and blessings that God wants to send to us. In all things we must trust in God and know that He will meet our needs in His time and in His way, which is perfect.

Suggested Prayer:

God, help me to realize that there is always a purpose to your methods. In times where I may find myself in situations of great need, helplessness or hopelessness help me to fully rely on, and trust in, your absolute power and love for me. Help me to know that despite my imperfections, weakness and inability that you will, and are always, working on my behalf.

Additional Biblical References:

Matthew 7:7 Ask and it will be given to you; seek and you will find; knock and the door will be opened to you.

Mark 11:24 Therefore I tell you, whatever you ask for in prayer, believe that you have received it, and it will be yours.

Philippians 4:12-13 I know how to be brought low, and I know how to abound. In any and every circumstance, I have learned the secret of facing plenty and hunger, abundance and need. I can do all things through Him who strengthens me.

Day 11

BIBLICAL MEDITATION TOPIC

God's Faithfulness

"Faithful is He who calls you, and He also will bring it to pass."
~1 Thessalonians 5:24

OPENING MEDITATION: 2 - 5 MINUTES
BIBLICAL MEDITATION: 5 - 15 MINUTES
CLOSING MEDITATION: 3 - 10 MINUTES

Quick Reference Guide: Biblical Meditation Instructions

Begin the opening meditation by quieting your thoughts in order to attach yourself more firmly to God.

Read the biblical meditations. Reflect upon how the topic pertains to your life or current circumstances.

Close the biblical meditations by focusing on what action(s) God may be requiring of you. Seek solutions in accordance with what God is calling you to do. Suggested prayers are provided to aid in this process.

If desired, read the section containing additional biblical references pertaining to the selected topic.

Day 11: God's Faithfulness

Faithfulness is a part of God's nature. He is steadfast, reliable and unwavering. In order to understand this truth we need only to look to the Bible, which affirms, "Jesus Christ is the same yesterday and today and forever" (Hebrews 13:8).

God's faithfulness is powerful and protects us from evil. "For the wrath of God is revealed from heaven against all ungodliness and unrighteousness of men, who by their unrighteousness suppress the truth" (Lamentations 3:22-23).

God's faithfulness provides us with endurance to address the various temptations that confront us. "Let us hold fast the confession of our hope without wavering, for He who promised is faithful" (Hebrews 10:23).

As a result of His faithfulness God is just and forgiving of our sins and unrighteousness. God's faithfulness sanctifies us, which is the process of completely separating us from the process of evil by changing, shaping and transforming us into His likeness.

God's faithfulness to us is a gift through which we are granted love, joy, peace, patience, kindness, goodness, faithfulness.

In recognition of and gratitude for God's grace, we too, are called to be people of faith.

Suggested Prayer:

God, thank you for your faithfulness that protects, loves, guides, fulfills and redeems me. God, help me to become a mirror of your greatness so that, I may become the person of faith that you call me to be.

Additional Biblical References:

>**Romans 3:3-4** What then? If some did not believe, their unbelief will not nullify the faithfulness of God, will it? May it never be! Rather, let God be found true, though every man be found a liar, as it is written, "THAT YOU MAY BE JUSTIFIED IN YOUR WORDS, AND PREVAIL WHEN YOU ARE JUDGED."

>**Acts 13:32-33** "And we preach to you the good news of the promise made to the fathers, that God has fulfilled this promise to our children in that He raised up Jesus, as it is also written in the second Psalm, 'YOU ARE MY SON; TODAY I HAVE BEGOTTEN YOU'."

>**Deuteronomy 7:9** Know therefore that the LORD your God is God, the faithful God who keeps covenant and steadfast love with those who love him and keep his commandments, to a thousand generations.

Day 12

BIBLICAL MEDITATION TOPIC
God's Grace

"Each one should use whatever gift he has received to serve others, faithfully administering God's grace in its various forms."
~1 Peter 4:10

OPENING MEDITATION: 2 - 5 MINUTES
BIBLICAL MEDITATION: 5 - 15 MINUTES
CLOSING MEDITATION: 3 - 10 MINUTES

Quick Reference Guide: Biblical Meditation Instructions

Begin the opening meditation by quieting your thoughts in order to attach yourself more firmly to God.

Read the biblical meditations. Reflect upon how the topic pertains to your life or current circumstances.

Close the biblical meditations by focusing on what action(s) God may be requiring of you. Seek solutions in accordance with what God is calling you to do. Suggested prayers are provided to aid in this process.

If desired, read the section containing additional biblical references pertaining to the selected topic.

Day 12: God's Grace

Grace is God's unmerited favor. It is a gift that God has bestowed upon us. It is not one that we deserve or are able to earn in any way. Rather, it is a precious gift that God gives us as a result of His unconditional love for us. "For it is by grace you have been saved, through faith--and this not from yourselves, it is the gift of God--not by works, so that no one can boast" (Ephesians 2:8-9).

Grace is a dominant theme throughout the Bible. Consider the various types of grace that God grants us:

> **Common grace** - the offer of salvation that God extends to all humankind;
>
> **Saving grace** - the rich inheritance that we receive through Christ that grants us salvation, redemption and forgiveness for our sins;
>
> **Securing grace** - God's benevolence through which Christians are kept secure;
>
> **Sanctifying grace** - the process of growth and maturity through which Christians strive to lead a more Christlike existence;
>
> **Serving grace** - the manifestation of the unique gifts that God gives each of us to serve and be blessings in manner that He might be known;
>
> **Sustaining grace** - the protection, the comfort, the ability to endure that God gives us, especially, during times of suffering, adversity or need.

God adopted us and predestined us to a rich inheritance through Jesus Christ. God's grace allows us a better understanding of who God is and His purpose for our lives.

Suggested Prayer:

God, thank you for your outpouring of grace into my life. Even though I have not earned it, please help me to be worthy of it so that I may grow in my faith and spiritual maturity, and through my actions, bring others to know your glory.

Additional Biblical References:

> **Romans 3:20-24** For by works of the law no human being will be justified in His sight, since through the law comes knowledge of sin. But now the righteousness of God has been manifested apart from the law, although the Law and the Prophets bear witness to it — the righteousness of God through faith in Jesus Christ for all who believe. For there is no distinction: for all have sinned and fall short of the glory of God, and are justified by His grace as a gift, through the redemption that is in Christ Jesus.

> **Hebrews 4:16** Let us then with confidence draw near to the throne of grace, that we may receive mercy and find grace to help in time of need.

Day 12: God's Grace

Acts 20:24 But I do not account my life of any value nor as precious to myself, if only I may finish my course and the ministry that I received from the Lord Jesus, to testify to the gospel of the grace of God.

DAY 13

BIBLICAL MEDITATION TOPIC
God's Will

"The world and its desires pass away, but whoever does the will of God lives forever."
~1 John 2:17

OPENING MEDITATION: 2 - 5 MINUTES
BIBLICAL MEDITATION: 5 - 15 MINUTES
CLOSING MEDITATION: 3 - 10 MINUTES

QUICK REFERENCE GUIDE: BIBLICAL MEDITATION INSTRUCTIONS

Begin the opening meditation by quieting your thoughts in order to attach yourself more firmly to God.

Read the biblical meditations. Reflect upon how the topic pertains to your life or current circumstances.

Close the biblical meditations by focusing on what action(s) God may be requiring of you. Seek solutions in accordance with what God is calling you to do. Suggested prayers are provided to aid in this process.

If desired, read the section containing additional biblical references pertaining to the selected topic.

Day 13: God's Will

While we may find things like God's wisdom and God's timing to be mysterious, other things such as God's will are made known to us.

In Deuteronomy 19:29 we see "The secret things belong to the LORD our God, but the things revealed belong to us and to our children forever, that we may follow all the words of this law." When we refer to God's will we refer to two things: God's will for humanity and God's plan for our lives.

The Bible reveals both.

In 1 Timothy 2:4 the Bible tells us that God's will for humanity is for "…all people to be saved and to come to the knowledge of the truth." Furthermore, Romans 8:29 tells us that it is God's will for us to be "conformed to the image of His Son". This was predestined by God.

God also has a specific plan for each of our lives. This varies for each person and is in accordance with the individual gifts and talents that God has granted us. Romans 11:29 affirms "…for God's gifts and his call are irrevocable" and Romans 8:28 "And we know that for those who love God all things work together for good, for those who are called according to his purpose."

So how can we know when we are doing the doing the will of God? The Bible gives us instruction.

"Believe, and Have Eternal life" **Jn 6:40**
"Praise and Give Him Glory" **Eph 1: 5-12**
"Live in His Grace" **Eph 5:1-20**
"Be Obedient to the Word of God" **Eph 6:5-8**
"Give Graciously" **2 Cor 8:1-7**
"Pray Without Ceasing" **1 Thess 5:11-18**
"Continue To Do What Is Right." **1 Pet 2:15**
"Keep Sane and Sober" **1 Pet 4:1-19**
"Bear Fruit In Good Work" **Col 1:9-12**
"Be His Servant" **Col 4:12**
"Do Not Be Conformed to the Ways of the World" 1 **Jn 2:15-17**
"Hear Your Calling According To His Purpose" **Rom 8:27-31**
"Do Not Repay Evil For Evil, Overcome Evil With Good" **Rom12:1-21**
"Pray For & Try To Save Your Brothers" **Rom 15:30-33 & Matt 18: 11-14**
"Avoid Immorality, Be Sanctified" 1 **Thess 4:1-8**
"Be Careful And Wise" **Eph 5-17**

God's nature is to reveal Himself. He makes His will known to all who seek Him. God wants us to know and do His will. The more we are obedient and strive to understand and do God's will, the more God is able to reveal to us.

Suggested Prayer:

God, thank you for making your will known through your unchanging Word and graciousness. I pray to know Your will more profoundly and to give You glory by fulfilling Your plan for my life.

Additional Biblical References:

John 6:45 It is written in the Prophets: "They will all be taught by God." Everyone who has heard the Father and learned from him comes to me.

Psalm 16:11 You make known to me the path of life; you will fill me with joy in your presence, with eternal pleasures at your right hand.

Mark 3:34-35 And looking about at those who sat around him, he said, "Here are my mother and my brothers! For whoever does the will of God, he is my brother and sister and mother."

DAY 14

BIBLICAL MEDITATION TOPIC
God's Love

"The Lord appeared to him from far away. I have loved you with an everlasting love; therefore I have continued my faithfulness to you."
–Jeremiah 31:3

OPENING MEDITATION: 2 - 5 MINUTES
BIBLICAL MEDITATION: 5 - 15 MINUTES
CLOSING MEDITATION: 3 - 10 MINUTES

Quick Reference Guide: Biblical Meditation Instructions

Begin the opening meditation by quieting your thoughts in order to attach yourself more firmly to God.

Read the biblical meditations. Reflect upon how the topic pertains to your life or current circumstances.

Close the biblical meditations by focusing on what action(s) God may be requiring of you. Seek solutions in accordance with what God is calling you to do. Suggested prayers are provided to aid in this process.

If desired, read the section containing additional biblical references pertaining to the selected topic.

Day 14: God's Love

God's love for us is the highest form of love that exists. We have not, nor could we ever, earn it. Rather, it is given to us as a result of God's grace and God's nature. God's love is unconditional and everlasting. The Bible demonstrates the scope of God's love.

> …in all these things we are more than conquerors through him who loved us. For I am sure that neither death nor life, nor angels nor rulers, nor things present nor things to come, nor powers, nor height nor depth, nor anything else in all creation, will be able to separate us from the love of God in Christ Jesus our Lord (Romans 8:37-39).

Indeed, in John 3:16, we are reminded that God loved us so much that "he gave his only Son, that whoever believes in Him should not perish but have eternal life…"

God loves us despite our disobedience, weaknesses and regardless of our imperfections. God's love is agape love – unconditional, compassionate, pure and self-sacrificing.

Neither God, nor His love, is distant from us. His love is active. God loves us as a true parent loves a child - guiding us, protecting us, and when necessary, even disciplining us.

God's love transforms and sanctifies us. Through God's love we know God because He is the source of love. John 4:16 reminds us "...we have come to know and to believe the love that God has in us. God is love, and the one who resides in love resides in God, and God in them."

Suggested Prayer:

Thank you for your loving nature. Thank you for loving me unconditionally. I pray to grow and be transformed more and more each day so that through my actions, and my testimony, I may show love to others.

Additional Biblical References:

> **John 4:9-10** By this the love of God is revealed in us: that God has sent his one and only Son into the world so that we may live through him. In this is love: not that we have loved God, but that he loved us and sent his Son to be the atoning sacrifice for our sins.

> **Romans 8:39** Nor height, nor depth, nor anything else in creation will be able to separate us from the love of God in Christ Jesus our Lord.

> **Zephaniah 3:17** The LORD your God is in your midst, a mighty one who will save; he will rejoice over you with gladness; he will quiet you by his love; he will exult over you with loud singing.

Day 15:	Blessings	111
Day 16:	Confidence	117
Day 17:	Determination	123
Day 18:	Courage	129
Day 19:	Integrity	135
Day 20:	Healing	141
Day 21:	Faith	147

WEEK 3

BIBLICAL MEDITATION TOPIC
Because He Is, We Are.

During the second week of our biblical meditations we contemplated God's amazing attributes. We saw that God is unrivaled, unparalleled, unlimited and unconditional in all that He is and all that He does.

We saw too, that God uses His might on our behalf. This He does because He loves us unconditionally. He is love. Through His love and His grace, God sanctifies and transforms us. We are reminded that He loved us before we were born. God created us in His image. He predestined us for greatness. God made the ultimate sacrifice for us. In this next section we focus on the amazing attributes that we as children of God, created in His awesome likeness, possess.

DAY 15

BIBLICAL MEDITATION TOPIC

Blessings

"Taste and see that the Lord is good; blessed is the one who takes refuge in him."
~Psalms 34:8

OPENING MEDITATION: 2 - 5 MINUTES
BIBLICAL MEDITATION: 5 - 15 MINUTES
CLOSING MEDITATION: 3 - 10 MINUTES

Quick Reference Guide: Biblical Meditation Instructions

Begin the opening meditation by quieting your thoughts in order to attach yourself more firmly to God.

Read the biblical meditations. Reflect upon how the topic pertains to your life or current circumstances.

Close the biblical meditations by focusing on what action(s) God may be requiring of you. Seek solutions in accordance with what God is calling you to do. Suggested prayers are provided to aid in this process.

If desired, read the section containing additional biblical references pertaining to the selected topic.

DAY 15: BLESSINGS

Blessings may come after, or even during, periods of great trial. In such instances, it may be hard to recognize the blessing as such. In order to understand how truly blessed we are, it is important to understand what the Bible says about blessings.

There are over 7000 references to blessings or being blessed throughout the Bible. The New Testament, for example, defines the word blessings as happiness. God's generosity is often noted. Being blessed, however, extends far beyond mere material possessions.

The Bible notes that blessed are those people who receive the corrective and guiding love of God. Even God's chastisement is a blessing. It should be considered an expression of love comparable to that of a parent who disciplines their child to protect them from harm and propel them toward their best.

> Blessed is the man whom God corrects; so do not despise the discipline of the Almighty (Job 5:17).

Additionally, the Bible notes that blessed are those who love and fear God.

> Blessed is the man who does not walk in the counsel of the wicked or stand in the way of sinners or sit in the seat

of mockers. But his delight is in the law of the LORD, and on his law he meditates day and night. He is like a tree planted by streams of water, which yields its fruit in season and whose leaf does not wither. Whatever he does prospers (Psalm 1:1-3).

Ultimately, however, we are most blessed by the offer of salvation that was extended through us through Jesus Christ. Through His sacrifice on the cross Jesus mended the relationship between God and mankind.

Suggested Prayer:

Thank you for the abundance of blessings that you have bestowed upon me. Guide me God, and help me to become a blessing in the lives of others.

Additional Biblical References:

James 1:12 Blessed is the man who remains steadfast under trial, for when he has stood the test he will receive the crown of life, which God has promised to those who love him.

Deuteronomy 7:13 He will love you, bless you, and multiply you. He will also bless the fruit of your womb and the fruit of your ground, your grain and your wine and your oil, the increase of your herds and the young of your flock, in the land that he swore to your fathers to give you.

2 Chronicles 1:11-12 God answered Solomon, "Because this was in your heart, and you have not asked possessions, wealth, honor, or the life of those who hate you, and have not even asked long life, but have asked wisdom and knowledge for yourself that you may govern my people over whom I have made you king, and knowledge are granted to you. I will also give you riches, possessions, and honor, such as none of the kings had who were before you, and none after you shall have the like."

DAY 16

BIBLICAL MEDITATION TOPIC

Confidence

*"So we can confidently say, 'The Lord is my helper;
I will not fear; what can man do to me?'"*
~Hebrews 13:6

OPENING MEDITATION: 2 - 5 MINUTES
BIBLICAL MEDITATION: 5 - 15 MINUTES
CLOSING MEDITATION: 3 - 10 MINUTES

QUICK REFERENCE GUIDE: BIBLICAL MEDITATION INSTRUCTIONS

Begin the opening meditation by quieting your thoughts in order to attach yourself more firmly to God.

Read the biblical meditations. Reflect upon how the topic pertains to your life or current circumstances.

Close the biblical meditations by focusing on what action(s) God may be requiring of you. Seek solutions in accordance with what God is calling you to do. Suggested prayers are provided to aid in this process.

If desired, read the section containing additional biblical references pertaining to the selected topic.

Day 16: Confidence

Confidence is a recurring theme in the Bible. It is also a highly sought after trait in today's society. To understand, in what manner believers are called to be confident, it is important to understand what the Bible has to say about this topic.

Confidence can be both negative and positive. In a negative context, confidence is an expression of arrogance or pride. It revolves around relying on our social class, educational or professional background, heredity, looks or other such attributes.

Such things are completely inconsequential to God. Such things do not make us more acceptable to God. We are reminded in Acts 10:34 "So Peter opened his mouth and said: 'Truly I understand that God shows no partiality'".

To place confidence in such attributes is to place things or persons, ourselves included, at the center of everything. To do so, is a destructive practice destined to lead to disappointment and potentially cause great harm to others and our relationship with God.

> "Stop regarding man in whose nostrils is breath, for of what account is he" (Isaiah 2:22)?

> "Whoever trusts in his own mind is a fool, but he who walks in wisdom will be delivered" (Proverbs 28:26).

God does, however, bless us with special talents and gifts. When we use these talents and gifts to glorify God and do his work, He equips us with the knowledge and resources necessary to ensure its success.

In this we can, and should, have confidence. King David, provides a perfect example. Although highly regarded, King David took no credit for his accomplishments instead attributing them all to God with gratitude, unwavering faith and confidence. Psalm 16 illustrate that point:

> Keep me safe, my God,
> for in you I take refuge.
> I say to the Lord, "You are my Lord;
> apart from you I have no good thing."
> I say of the holy people who are in the land,
> "They are the noble ones in whom is all my delight."
> Those who run after other gods will suffer more and more.
> I will not pour out libations of blood to such gods
> or take up their names on my lips.
> Lord, you alone are my portion and my cup;
> you make my lot secure.
> The boundary lines have fallen for me in pleasant places;
> surely I have a delightful inheritance.
> I will praise the Lord, who counsels me;
> even at night my heart instructs me.
> I keep my eyes always on the Lord.
> With him at my right hand, I will not be shaken.

> Therefore my heart is glad and my tongue rejoices;
> my body also will rest secure,
> because you will not abandon me to the realm of the dead,
> nor will you let your faithful one see decay.
> You make known to me the path of life;
> you will fill me with joy in your presence,
> with eternal pleasures at your right hand.

Most importantly, we can have confidence in our relationship with God and His mercy, grace and love. We can have absolute confidence in His sovereignty and that He uses it on our behalf. We can know that we are called, protected, loved and saved.

Suggested Prayer:

God, please help to remain steadfast in my faith and place all my confidence in you and all the promises that you have made for my life.

Additional Biblical References:

> **Hebrews 4:16** Let us then with confidence draw near to the throne of grace, that we may receive mercy and find grace to help in time of need.

Philippians 3:3 For we are the circumcision, who worship by the Spirit of God and glory in Christ Jesus and put no confidence in the flesh.

Proverbs 14:16 One who is wise is cautious and turns away from evil, but a fool is reckless and careless.

DAY 17

BIBLICAL MEDITATION TOPIC
Determination

"And let us not grow weary of doing good, for in due season we will reap, if we do not give up."
~Galatians 6:9

OPENING MEDITATION: 2 - 5 MINUTES
BIBLICAL MEDITATION: 5 - 15 MINUTES
CLOSING MEDITATION: 3 - 10 MINUTES

Quick Reference Guide: Biblical Meditation Instructions

Begin the opening meditation by quieting your thoughts in order to attach yourself more firmly to God.

Read the biblical meditations. Reflect upon how the topic pertains to your life or current circumstances.

Close the biblical meditations by focusing on what action(s) God may be requiring of you. Seek solutions in accordance with what God is calling you to do. Suggested prayers are provided to aid in this process.

If desired, read the section containing additional biblical references pertaining to the selected topic.

Day 17: Determination

Determination is the opposite of fear doubt and worry. It requires persistence in our pursuit of understanding God's Word and doing God's will. It requires perseverance in the face of obstacles and barriers. The Bible shows us that it is also a test our faith.

We are instructed to remain steadfast in our endurance of tough circumstances. Our determination must be a commitment to embrace God's presence and power in our lives. We must root our determination in much more than a desire to simply excel or succeed. To do so we must set ourselves toward Godly pursuits,

> Do you not know that in a race all the runners run, but only one receives the prize? So run that you may obtain it. Every athlete exercises self-control in all things. They do it to receive a perishable wreath, but we an imperishable. So I do not run aimlessly; I do not box as one beating the air. But I discipline my body and keep it under control, lest after preaching to others I myself should be disqualified (1 Corinthians 9:24-27).

The Bible warns that we may face trials that will attempt to distract or discourage us. "Evil men plot against the godly and viciously attack them" Psalm 37:12. As a result we must have righteous determination.

Righteous determination is rooted in a earnest desire and dedication to do God's work and to live

His word daily. We must fully rely on Him. Knowing that for us God made the ultimate sacrifice and gave His only son Jesus Christ. We must trust in God's love and His wisdom to guide our paths.

> For I know the plans I have for you, declares the LORD, plans for welfare and not for evil, to give you a future and a hope (Jeremiah 29:11).

Suggested Prayer:

Father, help me to remain strong even during the most trying times. When I feel I am at my weakest point and no longer able to fight, help me to remember that it is You who strengthens me and that You are always at my side guiding me, loving me and preparing me for victory.

Additional Biblical References:

2 Thessalonians 3:13 As for you, brothers, do not grow weary in doing good.

1 Timothy 6:12 Fight the good fight of the faith. Take hold of the eternal life to which you were called and about which you made the good confession in the presence of many witnesses.

Day 17: Determination

2 Timothy 4:7-8 I have fought the good fight, I have finished the race, I have kept the faith. Now there is in store for me the crown of righteousness, which the Lord, the righteous Judge, will award to me on that day—and not only to me, but also to all who have longed for his appearing.

DAY 18

BIBLICAL MEDITATION TOPIC
Courage

"Be on your guard; stand firm in the faith; be men of courage; be strong."
~1 Corinthians 16:13

OPENING MEDITATION: 2 - 5 MINUTES
BIBLICAL MEDITATION: 5 - 15 MINUTES
CLOSING MEDITATION: 3 - 10 MINUTES

Quick Reference Guide: Biblical Meditation Instructions

Begin the opening meditation by quieting your thoughts in order to attach yourself more firmly to God.

Read the biblical meditations. Reflect upon how the topic pertains to your life or current circumstances.

Close the biblical meditations by focusing on what action(s) God may be requiring of you. Seek solutions in accordance with what God is calling you to do. Suggested prayers are provided to aid in this process.

If desired, read the section containing additional biblical references pertaining to the selected topic.

Day 18: Courage

Courage is the opposite of fear. From Abraham to the Apostles, there are many examples throughout the Bible of people being commanded to "fear not".

During the time of the Israelites and Philistines, God empowered David, a young small boy, to defeat the menacing and violent giant, Goliath. David's own brothers, and even the king's men, were afraid to take on such a massive foe. David understood "I can do all things through Him who strengthens me" (Philippians 4:13).

Throughout the books of Acts we see that John and Peter faced constant persecution, and even the threat of death, while doing God's work.

Despite the opposition from powerful religious leaders they continued to glorify God. Courageously they answered "Whether it be right in the sight of God to harken unto you more than unto God, judge ye, but we cannot but speak of the things we have heard and seen" (Acts 4:19-20).

We are reminded that as Gods people, we are covered by His protection. God Himself is the reason that we are able to be brave and courageous in all things. We are to have confidence in God's sovereignty and knowledge that if we have courage, and act in faith, God's plan for us will not be thwarted.

> Have no fear of sudden disaster or of the ruin that overtakes the wicked, for the Lord will be your confidence and will keep your foot from being snared (Proverbs 3: 25-26).

God also empowers us with His Word, the strongest all weapons, to confront any obstacles or evils that we may face

> For the word of God is alive and active. Sharper than any double-edged sword, it penetrates even to dividing soul and spirit, joints and marrow; it judges the thoughts and attitudes of the heart Hebrews 4:12.

Suggested Prayer:

God, please remove any remaining spirit of doubt, fear or uncertainty so that I may boldly do your work and will in all things with unwavering confidence and courage.

Additional Biblical References:

> **Psalms 31:24** Be of good courage, and he shall strengthen your heart, all ye that hope in the LORD.

Day 18: Courage

1 Chronicles 28:20 David also said to Solomon his son, "Be strong and courageous, and do the work. Do not be afraid or discouraged, for the LORD God, my God is with you.

Joshua 1:5-9 "No man shall be able to stand before you all the days of your life. Just as I was with Moses, so I will be with you. I will not leave you or forsake you. Be strong and courageous, for you shall cause this people to inherit the land that I swore to their fathers to give them. Only be strong and very courageous, being careful to do according to all the law that Moses my servant commanded you. Have I not commanded you? Be strong and courageous."

DAY
19

BIBLICAL MEDITATION TOPIC
Integrity

"For we aim at what is honorable not only in the Lord's sight but also in the sight of man."
~2 Corinthians 8:21

OPENING MEDITATION: 2 - 5 MINUTES
BIBLICAL MEDITATION: 5 - 15 MINUTES
CLOSING MEDITATION: 3 - 10 MINUTES

Quick Reference Guide: Biblical Meditation Instructions

Begin the opening meditation by quieting your thoughts in order to attach yourself more firmly to God.

Read the biblical meditations. Reflect upon how the topic pertains to your life or current circumstances.

Close the biblical meditations by focusing on what action(s) God may be requiring of you. Seek solutions in accordance with what God is calling you to do. Suggested prayers are provided to aid in this process.

If desired, read the section containing additional biblical references pertaining to the selected topic.

Day 19: Integrity

Integrity is a recurrent theme throughout the Bible. It is used synonymously with honesty and truth. Examples of integrity are offered in various passages throughout the Old Testament and New Testament.

> And as for you, if you will walk before Me, as David your father walked, with integrity of heart and uprightness, doing according to all that I have commanded you, and keeping My statutes and my rules, then I will establish your royal throne over Israel forever, as I promised David your father, saying, 'You shall not lack a man on the throne of Israel' (1 Kings 9:4-5).

> And the LORD said to Satan, "Have you considered my servant Job, that there is none like him on the earth, a blameless and upright man, who fears God and turns away from evil? He still holds fast his integrity, although you incited me against him to destroy him without reason" (Job 2:3).

> Show yourself in all respects to be a model of good works, and in your teaching show integrity, dignity, and sound speech that cannot be condemned, so that an opponent may be put to shame, having nothing evil to say about us (Titus 2:7-8).

Philippians 4:8 offers the following definition of integrity"…whatever is true, whatever is noble, whatever is right, whatever is pure, whatever is lovely, whatever is admirable—if anything is excellent or praiseworthy…"

We see that Integrity is much more highly valued than status, education or any worldly possessions.

As believers we are commanded to lead a life filled with integrity. To do so we must accept God and seek to live as Jesus lived. When we do so, we are reborn in Christ. This allows us to partake of his divine nature. 2 Corinthians 5:7 reminds us "Therefore, if anyone is in Christ, he is a new creation. The old has passed away; behold, the new has come."

Jesus is perfect. Integrity is inherent in His nature. When we are in Christ, the perfection of His integrity is extended to us as well.

Suggested Prayer:

Lord, please help me to develop and maintain integrity that is so strong and incorruptible that is evident to, and serves as an example, for others.

Additional Biblical References:

> **Proverbs 2:6-8** For the LORD gives wisdom; from his mouth come knowledge and understanding; he stores up sound wisdom for the upright; he is a shield to those who walk in integrity, guarding the paths of justice and watching over the way of his saints.

Day 19: Integrity

Psalm 26:1-3 Vindicate me, O LORD, for I have walked in my integrity, and I have trusted in the LORD without wavering. Prove me, O LORD, and try me; test my heart and my mind. For your steadfast love is before my eyes, and I walk in your faithfulness.

1 Timothy 2:1-4 I exhort therefore, that, first of all, supplications, prayers, intercessions, and giving of thanks, be made for all men; For kings, and for all that are in authority; that we may lead a quiet and peaceable life in all godliness and honesty. For this is good and acceptable in the sight of God our Saviour; Who will have all men to be saved, and to come unto the knowledge of the truth.

DAY 20

BIBLICAL MEDITATION TOPIC

Healing

"Heal me, O Lord, and I shall be healed; save me, and I shall be saved, for you are my praise."
~Jeremiah 17:14

OPENING MEDITATION: 2 - 5 MINUTES
BIBLICAL MEDITATION: 5 - 15 MINUTES
CLOSING MEDITATION: 3 - 10 MINUTES

QUICK REFERENCE GUIDE: BIBLICAL MEDITATION INSTRUCTIONS

Begin the opening meditation by quieting your thoughts in order to attach yourself more firmly to God.

Read the biblical meditations. Reflect upon how the topic pertains to your life or current circumstances.

Close the biblical meditations by focusing on what action(s) God may be requiring of you. Seek solutions in accordance with what God is calling you to do. Suggested prayers are provided to aid in this process.

If desired, read the section containing additional biblical references pertaining to the selected topic.

Day 20: Healing

Healing may be spiritual or physical in nature. Often it is physical healing that we desire, and indeed, for which we pray. It is important, however, to understand what the Bible says about healing.

Regarding this, we see three main points. First, the Bible tells us that the Word of God heals. Second, we see that God sent us complete healing through His living Word, Jesus Christ. Third, He has granted believers the gift to heal.

Yet, there are moments when healing does not occur. For this, the Bible offers the following explanations. Early Christians believed unwaveringly not only in the power to be healed but in the ability granted to them, through Jesus Christ, to heal others. Today, mankind is riddled by a lack of faith. Doubt, fear, stress and distrust are common, even among Christians. These things do immeasurable harm to our body and often hinder God's presence in our lives.

God has given us free will. As a result of sin many harmful and even toxic things exist that undermine the health and wholeness that God desires for us. God works miracles in our lives. However, when and how he chooses to do so often defies our limited understanding. Healing, as stated earlier, can also be spiritual in nature.

Spiritual healing refers to being saved and forgiven. Often biblical texts that are quoted in regards to healing, actually refer to spiritual as opposed to physical healing:

> But he was pierced for our transgressions; he was crushed for our iniquities; upon him was the chastisement that brought us peace, and with his wounds we are healed (Isiah 53:5).

Furthermore, regarding this verse 1Peter 2:24 explains "He himself bore our sins in his body on the tree that we might die to sin and live to righteousness. By his wounds you have been healed."

Ultimately, it is spiritual healing that guarantees that we will one day shed sickness, disease and earthly limitations. It is as a result of spiritual healing that will experience the full glory of heaven.

Suggested Prayer:

God, help me to be happy, whole and healed physically, emotionally and spiritually."

Additional Biblical References:

2 Corinthians 12:8-9 Three different times I begged the Lord to take it away. Each time he said, "My grace is all you need. My power works best in weakness." So now I am glad to boast about my weaknesses, so that the power of Christ can work through me.

Matthew 9:28-29 They went right into the house where he was staying, and Jesus asked them, "Do you believe I can make you see?" "Yes, Lord," they told him, "we do." Then he touched their eyes and said, "Because of your faith, it will happen."

Mark 9:23 Jesus said unto him, If thou canst believe, all things [are] possible to him that believeth.

Day 21

BIBLICAL MEDITATION TOPIC
Faith

"Faith is the substance of things hoped for, the evidence of things not seen."
~Hebrews 11:1

OPENING MEDITATION: 2 - 5 MINUTES
BIBLICAL MEDITATION: 5 - 15 MINUTES
CLOSING MEDITATION: 3 - 10 MINUTES

Quick Reference Guide: Biblical Meditation Instructions

Begin the opening meditation by quieting your thoughts in order to attach yourself more firmly to God.

Read the biblical meditations. Reflect upon how the topic pertains to your life or current circumstances.

Close the biblical meditations by focusing on what action(s) God may be requiring of you. Seek solutions in accordance with what God is calling you to do. Suggested prayers are provided to aid in this process.

If desired, read the section containing additional biblical references pertaining to the selected topic.

Day 21: Faith

Faith empowers ordinary individuals to accomplish extraordinary feats. The Bible provides a multitude of such examples.

> By faith Noah, being warned of God of things not seen as yet, moved with fear, prepared an ark to the saving of his house; by the which he condemned the world, and became heir of the righteousness which is by faith (Hebrews 11:7).

> By faith Abraham, when he was tried, offered up Isaac: and he that had received the promises offered up his only begotten son, Of whom it was said, That in Isaac shall thy seed be called: Accounting that God was able to raise him up, even from the dead; from whence also he received him in a figure (Hebrews 11:17-19).

> By faith the harlot Rahab perished not with them that believed not, when she had received the spies with peace (Hebrews 11:31).

Faith makes us acceptable to God and ensures our salvation. It is an active unwavering trust, belief, confidence in and reliance upon God. It is a conscience decision to exalt God rather than worldly things in our lives. God, the life of, and subsequent loving sacrifice, of His son Jesus Christ must be the center of our faith to ensure our salvation and redemption.

> Choose this day whom you will serve…as for me and my house we will serve the Lord.

The Bible tells us that our good works, and the extent to which we help others, serve as evidence of our faith. James 2:18 affirms "I will show you my faith by my work." Faith also involves being obedient to God's Word and to the teachings of Jesus.

Faith, however, does not require perfection. In fact, there are times when our faith will be tested. The testing of our faith creates opportunities for us to grow in our relationship with God. James 1:2-4 tells us:

> Count it all joy, my brothers, when you meet trials of various kinds, for you know that the testing of your faith produces steadfastness. And let steadfastness have its full effect, that you may be perfect and complete, lacking in nothing.

As we encounter various trials and obstacles we must remember that God loves us and is always working on our behalf. Though all of His ways may not be known to us, we know that through our faith we are offered salvation. We know that through our faith we fully become His.

Suggested Prayer:

God, please help me to eliminate any fear or doubt that prevents me from having absolute faith and fully serving You. Help me to become more obedient so my faith is evident through the good works and fruits that I produce.

Additional Biblical References:

Luke 17:5 The apostles said to the Lord, "Increase our faith!" He replied, "If you have faith as small as a mustard seed, you can say to this mulberry tree, 'Be uprooted and planted in the sea,' and it will obey you."

1Peter 1:7-9 So that the proof of your faith, being more precious than gold which is perishable, even though tested by fire, may be found to result in praise and glory and honor at the revelation of Jesus Christ; and though you have not seen Him, you love Him, and though you do not see Him now, but believe in Him, you greatly rejoice with joy inexpressible and full of glory, obtaining as the outcome of your faith the salvation of your souls.

Ephesians 3:16-17 I pray that out of his glorious riches he may strengthen you with power through his Spirit in your inner being, so that Christ may dwell in your hearts through faith. And I pray that you, being rooted and established in love.

Day 22	Gentleness	155
Day 23	Generosity	161
Day 24	Forgiveness	167
Day 25	Tolerance	173
Day 26	Unity	179
Day 27	Evangelism	185
Day 28	Love	191

WEEK 4

BIBLICAL MEDITATION TOPIC
Great Power, Great Responsibility.

We saw in the preceding part of the biblical meditations that God calls and equips us to be extraordinary. As children of such an extraordinary Creator, determination, courage and blessings, are but a few of the attributes that we possess. God blesses us with these not only for own happiness and well-being but also so that we are able to be a blessing to others.

Just as God has shown us mercy, grace, and love, so to do we have responsibilities toward others. As we close our 28 days of biblical meditation we focus on fulfilling our duties toward others

DAY 22

BIBLICAL MEDITATION TOPIC

Gentleness

"Blessed are the gentle, for they shall inherit the earth."
~Matthew 5:5

OPENING MEDITATION: 2 - 5 MINUTES
BIBLICAL MEDITATION: 5 - 15 MINUTES
CLOSING MEDITATION: 3 - 10 MINUTES

Quick Reference Guide: Biblical Meditation Instructions

Begin the opening meditation by quieting your thoughts in order to attach yourself more firmly to God.

Read the biblical meditations. Reflect upon how the topic pertains to your life or current circumstances.

Close the biblical meditations by focusing on what action(s) God may be requiring of you. Seek solutions in accordance with what God is calling you to do. Suggested prayers are provided to aid in this process.

If desired, read the section containing additional biblical references pertaining to the selected topic.

Day 22: Gentleness

Gentleness is the 8th fruit of the spirit. It is often misinterpreted as being weak, timid or passive. On the contrary, however, we see that the most powerful biblical figures were gentle!

Consider the examples of Moses, Jesus and Paul.

Of Moses, the Bible says "Now the man Moses was very humble, more than all men who were on the face of the earth" (Numbers 12:3).

Moses faced great obstacles not only from his opponents but from those he was chosen to lead out of slavery in Egypt. He even faced opposition from within his family regarding his choice of an Ethiopian wife. Yet, he did the tremendous work that was entrusted to him without complaining or questioning God.

Though he was perfect and innocent of any wrongdoing, Jesus willingly bore the sins of the world so that we could have forgiveness from our transgressions and be granted salvation

> Surely He has borne our griefs And carried our sorrows; Yet we esteemed Him stricken, smitten by God, and afflicted. But He was wounded for our transgressions, He was bruised for our iniquities; The chastisement for our peace was upon Him, And by His stripes we are healed (Isaiah 53:4-5).

Through His gentleness Jesus exemplified self-sacrifice, concern and absolute love for others.

After his amazing transformation Paul faced great opposition to his work to spread Christianity. Paul's response to this opposition served as, and continues to serve as, an example to God's faithful servants, such as Titus, who were also facing many challenges as they obeyed their calling. Paul advises:

> "What do you prefer? Shall I come to you with a rod of discipline, or shall I come in love and with a gentle spirit?" (1 Corinthians 4:21).

> Therefore I, the prisoner for the Lord, urge you to walk worthy of the calling you have received, with all humility and gentleness, with patience, accepting one another in love, diligently keeping the unity of the Spirit with the peace that binds us (Ephesians 4:1-3).

> Opponents must be gently instructed, in the hope that God will grant them repentance leading them to a knowledge of the truth (2 Timothy 2:25).

Paul's gentleness required courage to stand against the opposition and continue to do the work that God called him to do without anger or aggression and, instead, to do so with compassion, humility, patience and gentleness.

From the above examples we see that not only are we to be gentle, we are to treat others gently.

Day 22: Gentleness

Gentleness as exemplified by Moses, Jesus and Paul is the complete opposite of weakness. Instead it is a demonstration of strength, especially under difficult circumstances. It is concern and deep caring for others to the extent that one is willing to make personal sacrifices or endure hardships. Gentleness is the embodiment of patience and forgiveness. It is an expression of humility and the complete submission or one's will and judgment to God. Gentleness requires absolute faith in both its embodiment and expression.

Suggested Prayer:

God, help me to truly develop a gentle spirit. Let courage, determination, selflessness and humility shine through me in order to do your work and illuminate the paths of others.

Additional Biblical References:

> **1 Peter 3:3-4** Do not let your adornment be merely outward—arranging the hair, wearing gold, or putting on fine apparel—rather let it be the hidden person of the heart, with the incorruptible beauty of a gentle and quiet spirit, which is very precious in the sight of God.

Galatians 5:22-23 But the fruit of the Spirit is love, joy, peace, long suffering, kindness, goodness, faithfulness, gentleness, self-control. Against such there is no law.

Matthew 11:28-30 Jesus said, "Come to Me, all you who labor and are heavy laden, and I will give you rest. Take My yoke upon you and learn from Me, for I am gentle and lowly in heart, and you will find rest for your souls. For My yoke is easy and My burden is light."

DAY 23

BIBLICAL MEDITATION TOPIC
Generosity

"Do not neglect to show hospitality to strangers, for thereby some have entertained angels unawares."
~Hebrews 13:2

OPENING MEDITATION: 2 - 5 MINUTES
BIBLICAL MEDITATION: 5 - 15 MINUTES
CLOSING MEDITATION: 3 - 10 MINUTES

***Quick Reference Guide: Biblical Meditation
Instructions***

Begin the opening meditation by quieting your thoughts in order to attach yourself more firmly to God.

Read the biblical meditations. Reflect upon how the topic pertains to your life or current circumstances.

Close the biblical meditations by focusing on what action(s) God may be requiring of you. Seek solutions in accordance with what God is calling you to do. Suggested prayers are provided to aid in this process.

If desired, read the section containing additional biblical references pertaining to the selected topic.

Day 23: Generosity

Generosity is heavily emphasized throughout the Bible and a key component of Jesus' ministry. In Isaiah 58:10-11 we are commanded

> "Feed the hungry! Help those in trouble! Then your light will shine out from the darkness, and the darkness around you shall be as bright as day. And the Lord will guide you continually, and satisfy you with all good things, and keep you healthy too; and you will be like a well-watered garden, like an ever-flowing spring.

Generosity is, indeed, an essential component of faith. It involves the use of gifts, talents, time or wealth to do good works and in some way make the world a better a place. We all have something to give and we should share that which we are able in accordance with the grace and gifts given to us.

> We have different gifts, according to the grace given to each of us. If your gift is prophesying, then prophesy in accordance with your faith; if it is serving, then serve; if it is teaching, then teach; if it is to encourage, then give encouragement; if it is giving, then give generously; if it is to lead, do it diligently; if it is to show mercy, do it cheerfully (Romans 12:6-8).

True generosity is the embodiment of a Christlike existence. In order for this to be so, however, our generosity must not be prompted by a desire for recognition or acknowledgment but rather a genuine desire to help others.

> "So when you give to the poor, do not sound a trumpet before you, as the hypocrites do in the synagogues and in the streets, so that they may be honored by men. Truly I say to you, they have their reward in full. But when you give to the poor, do not let your left hand know what your right hand is doing, so that your giving will be in secret; and your Father who sees what is done in secret will reward you" (Matthew 6: 2-4).

True generosity does not exploit others nor does it allow the giver to be exploited. It is both a blessing to those who give as well as those who receive. In Acts 20:33-35, Paul reminds us:

> I coveted no one's silver or gold or apparel. You yourselves know that these hands ministered to my necessities and to those who were with me. In all things I have shown you that by working hard in this way we must help the weak and remember the words of the Lord Jesus, how he himself said, 'It is more blessed to give than to receive.'

Most importantly through our generosity to others, we can show gratitude to God for the many ways in which He blesses us.

> We want you to know, brothers, about the grace of God that has been given among the churches of Macedonia, for in a severe test of affliction, their abundance of joy and their extreme poverty have overflowed in a wealth of generosity on their part. For they gave according to their means, as I can testify, and beyond their means, of their own accord, begging us earnestly for the favor of taking part in the relief of the saints— and this, not as we expected, but they gave themselves first to the Lord and then by the will of God to us (2 Corinthians 8: 1-5).

Every instance of true generosity no matter how large or small is an act of faith. It is an expression of love.

Suggested Prayer:

God, help me to identify the gifts, talents and resources that I may use to be a blessing to others. Guide me so that every act of generosity reflects my faith and becomes an expression of your love.

Additional Biblical References:

>**Matthew 7:12** "So whatever you wish that others would do to you, do also to them, for this is the Law and the Prophets."
>
>**1 John 3:17** But if anyone has the world's goods and sees his brother in need, yet closes his heart against him, how does God's love abide in him?
>
>**2 Corinthians 9:7** Each one must give as he has decided in his heart, not reluctantly or under compulsion, for God loves a cheerful giver.

DAY 24

BIBLICAL MEDITATION TOPIC

Forgiveness

"Be kind to one another, tenderhearted, forgiving one another, as God in Christ forgave you."
~Ephesians 4:32

OPENING MEDITATION: 2 - 5 MINUTES
BIBLICAL MEDITATION: 5 - 15 MINUTES
CLOSING MEDITATION: 3 - 10 MINUTES

Q*UICK *R*EFERENCE *G*UIDE: *B*IBLICAL *M*EDITATION *INSTRUCTIONS

Begin the opening meditation by quieting your thoughts in order to attach yourself more firmly to God.

Read the biblical meditations. Reflect upon how the topic pertains to your life or current circumstances.

Close the biblical meditations by focusing on what action(s) God may be requiring of you. Seek solutions in accordance with what God is calling you to do. Suggested prayers are provided to aid in this process.

If desired, read the section containing additional biblical references pertaining to the selected topic.

Day 24: Forgiveness

Forgiveness is a concept with which many people struggle. However, it is essential to our well-being, salvation and faith. As a result it is a prominent theme in the Bible. In the Bible, forgiveness is centered around our forgiving others and God forgiving our sins.

The Bible commands us to forgive those who have wronged us in someway. When we forgive we release the person that has committed the offense from blame and allow God to deal with the matter. Forgiveness frees us from having to assume the responsibility of such burdens and, instead allows us to entrust it to God. Forgiveness frees us from anger, bitterness and rage.

The compassion that we demonstrate via the act of forgiveness, also frees the wrongdoer from guilt and creates an opportunity for the wrongdoer to someday be transformed.

Forgiveness, especially under extraordinary circumstances, can be quite challenging. It may even seem impossible. However, we are reminded in 2 Corinthians 2:5-8

> If anyone has caused grief, he has not so much grieved me as he has grieved all of you to some extent—not to put it too severely. The punishment inflicted on him by the majority is sufficient. Now instead, you ought to

> forgive and comfort him, so that he will not be overwhelmed by excessive sorrow. I urge you, therefore, to reaffirm your love for him.

We must continue to, and even repeatedly, forgive when necessary;

> Then Peter came to Jesus and asked, "Lord, how many times shall I forgive my brother when he sins against me? Up to seven times? "Jesus answered, "I tell you, not seven times, but seventy-seven times" (Matthew 18: 21-22).

Forgiveness is an act of faith that attests to our spiritual growth. It is evidence that we are choosing to live out the love of God in our lives. It is recognition of and thanks for God's forgiveness of our sins and the gift of salvation and redemption that was given to us through the sacrifice of Christ.

We must forgive others just as we have been forgiven.

Suggested Prayer:

Lord, help me to embody your love and grace, by truly learning to forgive others. Father, please heal and bless the person who has wronged me so that they too may truly be transformed.

Additional Biblical References:

Colossians 3:13 Bear with each other and forgive one another if any of you has a grievance against someone. Forgive as the Lord forgave you.

Ephesians 4:31-32 Get rid of all bitterness, rage and anger, brawling and slander, along with every form of malice. Be kind and compassionate to one another, forgiving each other, just as in Christ God forgave you.

Acts 7:59-60 While they were stoning him, Stephen prayed, "Lord Jesus, receive my spirit." Then he fell on his knees and cried out, "Lord, do not hold this sin against them." When he had said this, he fell asleep.

Day 25

BIBLICAL MEDITATION TOPIC
Tolerance

"Blessed are the peacemakers: for they shall be called the children of God."
~Matthew 5:9

OPENING MEDITATION: 2 - 5 MINUTES
BIBLICAL MEDITATION: 5 - 15 MINUTES
CLOSING MEDITATION: 3 - 10 MINUTES

Quick Reference Guide: Biblical Meditation Instructions

Begin the opening meditation by quieting your thoughts in order to attach yourself more firmly to God.

Read the biblical meditations. Reflect upon how the topic pertains to your life or current circumstances.

Close the biblical meditations by focusing on what action(s) God may be requiring of you. Seek solutions in accordance with what God is calling you to do. Suggested prayers are provided to aid in this process.

If desired, read the section containing additional biblical references pertaining to the selected topic.

Day 25: Tolerance

Tolerance is likened to patience, forbearance and even long-suffering throughout the Bible. We are commanded to be tolerant of others.

> You have heard that it was said, You shall love your neighbor and hate your enemy. But I say to you, Love your enemies and pray for those who persecute you, so that you may be sons of your Father who is in heaven. For he makes his sun rise on the evil and on the good, and sends rain on the just and on the unjust. For if you love those who love you, what reward do you have? Do not even the tax collectors do the same? And if you greet only your brothers, what more are you doing than others? Do not even the Gentiles do the same? You therefore must be perfect, as your heavenly Father is perfect (Matthew 5:43-47).

To be tolerant means being loving and considerate of those who differ from us. This, involves the application of principles that are central to the Christian faith such as patience and love. To do so, we should Focus on areas of agreement, things in common. Paul shows us:

> For though I am free from all men, I have made myself a slave to all, so that I may win more. To the Jews I became as a Jew, so that I might win Jews; to those who are under the Law, as under the Law though not being myself under the Law, so that I might win those who are under the Law; to those who are without law, as without law, though not being without the law of God but under the law of Christ, so that I might win those who are without law... (1 Corinthians 9:19-23).

Tolerance involves the acknowledgment that others have differing beliefs. This does not mean, however, that Christians must fully accept those beliefs as true. Rather it means

> ...you know that they breed quarrels. And the Lord's servant must not be quarrelsome but kind to everyone, able to teach, patiently enduring evil, correcting his opponents with gentleness. God may perhaps grant them repentance leading to a knowledge of the truth, and they may come to their senses and escape from the snare of the devil, after being captured by him to do his will (2 Timothy 2:23-26).

There are, however, instances where we must absolutely not be tolerant. We must actively shun evil or deliberate wrongdoing. King David provided an example:

> I will set no worthless thing before my eyes; I hate the work of those who fall away; It shall not fasten its grip on me. A perverse heart shall depart from me; I will know no evil. Whoever secretly slanders his neighbor, him I will destroy; No one who has a haughty look and an arrogant heart will I endure (Psalm 101:3-5).

Jesus was completely intolerant of evil:

> ...and he [Satan] said to Him, "All these things I will give You, if You fall down and worship me." Then Jesus said to him, "Go, Satan! For it is written, 'YOU SHALL WORSHIP THE LORD YOUR GOD, AND SERVE HIM ONLY'" (Matthew 4:9-10).

We must not deny truths that have been revealed to us. Nor must we allow the truth to be hidden or distorted in the name of tolerance. 1 Corinthians 13:6 teaches us "Love does not delight in evil but rejoices with the truth'

As we grow in our faith, we must strive everyday to become more Christlike. God has extended tolerance to us regardless of whether or not we have actually earned it. Therefore we must extend the same consideration to others.

> Therefore, as God's chosen people, holy and dearly loved, clothe yourselves with compassion, kindness, humility, gentleness and patience. Bear with each other and forgive one another if any of you has a grievance against someone. Forgive as the Lord forgave you (Colossians 3:12).

Suggested Prayer:

God, grant me the discernment necessary to know when and how to exercise tolerance.

Additional Biblical References:

> **Hebrews 12:14** Follow peace with all men, and holiness, without which no man shall see the Lord.

Roman 14:2 Now accept the one who is weak in faith, but not for the purpose of passing judgment on his opinions. One person has faith that he may eat all things, but he who is weak eats vegetables only. The one who eats is not to regard with contempt the one who does not eat, and the one who does not eat is not to judge the one who eats, for God has accepted him.

Corinthians 10:23 All things are lawful, but not all things are profitable. All things are lawful, but not all things edify.

DAY 26

BIBLICAL MEDITATION TOPIC

Unity

"How good and pleasant it is when brothers live together in unity."
~Psalm 133:1

OPENING MEDITATION: 2 - 5 MINUTES
BIBLICAL MEDITATION: 5 - 15 MINUTES
CLOSING MEDITATION: 3 - 10 MINUTES

QUICK REFERENCE GUIDE: BIBLICAL MEDITATION INSTRUCTIONS

Begin the opening meditation by quieting your thoughts in order to attach yourself more firmly to God.

Read the biblical meditations. Reflect upon how the topic pertains to your life or current circumstances.

Close the biblical meditations by focusing on what action(s) God may be requiring of you. Seek solutions in accordance with what God is calling you to do. Suggested prayers are provided to aid in this process.

If desired, read the section containing additional biblical references pertaining to the selected topic.

Day 26: Unity

Unity is a dominant and central theme in the Bible. As believers we are urged to be united.

> The body is a unit, though it is made up of many parts; and though all its parts are many, they form one body. So it is with Christ. For we were all baptized by one Spirit into one body--whether Jews or Greeks, slave or free--and we were all given the one Spirit to drink (1 Corinthians 12:12-13).

The Bible teaches us that unity is "good" and "pleasant" and that it is a consequence of faith. "And all that believed were together, and had all things common" (Acts 2:44).

Yet, unity seems difficult to achieve not only at the individual level but within the church as well. Paul explains that this results from being overly focused on our needs and desires rather than those of others. Selflessness, not selfishness, is the true evidence and result of our faith.

> For you are yet carnal. For in that there is among you envyings and strife and divisions, are you not carnal, and do you not walk according to men (1 Corinthians 3:3)?

As we grow in our faith, it is important that we strive to be more and more Christlike. Christ sacrificed Himself to atone for our sins, so that we might have salvation. Thus, we too, must also learn to consider the needs of others. Our actions, must be motivated, by care and concern for others.

> ...make my joy complete by being of the same mind, maintaining the same love, united in spirit, intent on one purpose. Do nothing from selfishness or empty conceit, but with humility of mind regard one another as more important than yourselves; do not merely look out for your own personal interests, but also for the interests of others (Philippians 2:2-4).

Unity with others and within the church occurs when we seek to develop our godliness, rather than focus on worldliness. Recognizing the needs of others, operating out of integrity and with complete humility produces peace, harmony and unity.

Unity allows us to do God's work here on earth.

> And he gave the apostles, the prophets, the evangelists, the shepherds and teachers, to equip the saints for the work of ministry, for building up the body of Christ, until we all attain to the unity of the faith and of the knowledge of the Son of God, to mature manhood, to the measure of the stature of the fullness of Christ (Ephesians 4:11-13).

Suggested Prayer:

God, let your grace and love shine through me so that I may be of one heart and soul with my brothers and sisters and that the fruits of my labor conquer division and produce peace and unity always.

Additional Biblical References:

Romans 12:16 Live in harmony with one another. Do not be proud, but be willing to associate with people of low position. Do not be conceited.

John 17:23 I in them and you in me. May they be brought to complete unity to let the world know that you sent me and have loved them even as you have loved me.

Ephesians 4:3 Make every effort to keep the unity of the Spirit through the bond of peace.

DAY 27

BIBLICAL MEDITATION TOPIC

Evangelism

"Then I heard the voice of the Lord saying, "Whom shall I send? And who will go for us?" And I said, "Here am I. Send me!"

~Isaiah 6:8

OPENING MEDITATION: 2 - 5 MINUTES
BIBLICAL MEDITATION: 5 - 15 MINUTES
CLOSING MEDITATION: 3 - 10 MINUTES

***Q*UICK *R*EFERENCE *G*UIDE: *B*IBLICAL *M*EDITATION *I*NSTRUCTIONS**

Begin the opening meditation by quieting your thoughts in order to attach yourself more firmly to God.

Read the biblical meditations. Reflect upon how the topic pertains to your life or current circumstances.

Close the biblical meditations by focusing on what action(s) God may be requiring of you. Seek solutions in accordance with what God is calling you to do. Suggested prayers are provided to aid in this process.

If desired, read the section containing additional biblical references pertaining to the selected topic.

Day 27: Evangelism

Evangelism spreads the good news of the life, death and resurrection of Jesus through which our loving Creator made redemption and salvation available to all of us.

> What therefore you worship as unknown, this I proclaim to you. The God who made the world and everything in it, being Lord of heaven and earth, does not live in temples made by man, nor is he served by human hands, as though he needed anything, since he himself gives to all mankind life and breath and everything. And he made from one man every nation of mankind to live on all the face of the earth, having determined allotted periods and the boundaries of their dwelling place, that they should seek God and perhaps feel their way toward him and find him. Yet he is actually not far from each one of us, for in him we live and move and have our being… (Acts 17:22-28).

The truth of God's presence and majesty surrounds us throughout the entirety of creation. God makes Himself known to us because He desires that we know and have a loving and profound relationship with Him. Yet, despite this many people are unaware of, reject or despise God because they have not had the opportunity to truly and meaningfully know Him or have been led astray by the misinformation or harmful actions of others.

As believers who have experienced God's grace, mercy and love in our lives we are tasked with the responsibility of spreading the message about God's love, mercy and gift of salvation to others.

> And Jesus came and said to them, "All authority in heaven and on earth has been given to me. Go therefore and make disciples of all nations, baptizing them in the name of the Father and of the Son and of the Holy Spirit, teaching them to observe all that I have commanded you. And behold, I am with you always, to the end of the age" (Matthew 28:18-20).

Evangelism may take many forms. This may include going door to door, serving within a church or some other capacity that utilizes the gifts and talents with which we have been blessed. Regardless of what form we choose we must, most importantly sanctify Christ in our hearts, so that we fully live and embody the Christian life. It is through our actions, even more so than our words, that the gospel can be shared. As Matthew 5:16 encourages us "In the same way, let your light shine before others, so that they may see your good works and give glory to your Father who is in heaven."

The duty of evangelism may seem daunting. However, we were given this responsibility and when we are obedient to God, we cannot fail. The Bible affirms:

> But you will receive power when the Holy Spirit has come upon you, and you will be my witnesses in Jerusalem and in all Judea and Samaria, and to the end of the earth (Acts 1:8).

> While Peter was reflecting on the vision, the Spirit said to him, "Behold, three men are looking for you. "But get up, go downstairs and accompany them without misgivings, for I have sent them Myself" (Acts 10:19-20).

> And the Lord said to Paul in the night by a vision, "Do not be afraid any longer, but go on speaking and do not be silent; for I am with you, and no man will attack you in order to harm you, for I have many people in this city." And he settled there a year and six months, teaching the word of God among them (Acts 18:9-11).

Not only do we bless others through our evangelism, we become blessed in the process. In addition to leading others to salvation, evangelism allows us to show our obedience and express our gratitude to God for all that He has given us.

> I thank Christ Jesus our Lord, who has strengthened me, because He considered me faithful, putting me into service, even though I was formerly a blasphemer and a persecutor and a violent aggressor Yet I was shown mercy because I acted ignorantly in unbelief; and the grace of our Lord was more than abundant, with the faith and love which are found in Christ Jesus (1 Timothy 1:12-14).

As we continue to share our faith, so we continue to grow in our faith.

Suggested Prayer:

God, strengthen me and guide my every action. Let the example of my life lead those who may be lost to better know your grace, mercy and love.

Additional Biblical References:

2 Corinthians 5:20 Therefore, we are ambassadors for Christ, as though God were making an appeal through us; we beg you on behalf of Christ, be reconciled to God.

Romans 10:10-15 For with the heart one believes and is justified, and with the mouth one confesses and is saved. For the Scripture says, "Everyone who believes in him will not be put to shame." For there is no distinction between Jew and Greek; for the same Lord is Lord of all, bestowing his riches on all who call on him. For "everyone who calls on the name of the Lord will be saved." How then will they call on him in whom they have not believed? And how are they to believe in him of whom they have never heard? And how are they to hear without someone preaching? And how are they to preach unless they are sent? As it is written, "How beautiful are the feet of those who preach the good news!"

Acts 4:20 For we cannot stop speaking about what we have seen and heard.

DAY 28

BIBLICAL MEDITATION TOPIC

Love

"We love because he first loved us."
~1 John 4:19

OPENING MEDITATION: 2 - 5 MINUTES
BIBLICAL MEDITATION: 5 - 15 MINUTES
CLOSING MEDITATION: 3 - 10 MINUTES

Quick Reference Guide: Biblical Meditation Instructions

Begin the opening meditation by quieting your thoughts in order to attach yourself more firmly to God.

Read the biblical meditations. Reflect upon how the topic pertains to your life or current circumstances.

Close the biblical meditations by focusing on what action(s) God may be requiring of you. Seek solutions in accordance with what God is calling you to do. Suggested prayers are provided to aid in this process.

If desired, read the section containing additional biblical references pertaining to the selected topic.

Day 28: Love

Love is the greatest of all actions. It is, in fact, one of the last commandments that Jesus gave before leaving the earth.

> The second is this, "You shall love your neighbor as yourself." There is no other commandment greater than these (Mark 12:31).

Our neighbors are more than those who reside near us or with whom we share proximity of beliefs, culture or social stature. Jesus explains that all of the people of all the world are our neighbors. This includes sinners and even our enemies.

Of sinners, we are reminded that we are all sinners and, despite our sins, love and forgiveness were extended to us.

> "If we say that we have no sin, we are deceiving ourselves and the truth is not in us. If we confess our sins, He is faithful and righteous to forgive us our sins and to cleanse us from all unrighteousness" (1 John 1:8-9).

Of our enemies, Jesus reminds us:

> "You have heard the law that says, 'Love your neighbor' and hate your enemy. But I say, love your enemies! Pray for those who persecute you! In that way, you will be acting as true children of your Father in heaven. For he gives his sunlight to both the evil and the good, and he sends rain on the just and the unjust alike. If you love only those who love you, what reward is there for that" (Matthew 5:43-46)?

We are to love in a manner that mirrors the love that God extends to us. Paul describes it in the following manner:

> Love is patient; love is kind; love is not envious or boastful or arrogant or rude. It does not insist on its own way; it is not irritable or resentful; it does not rejoice in wrongdoing, but rejoices in the truth. It bears all things, believes all things, hopes all things, endures all things. Love never ends (1 Corinthians 13:4-7).

The love that we show others must be an evident, not merely in our words but in the truth of our actions. This is something which that we are continuously commanded to do throughout the Bible. Furthermore, we are commanded to do so in a selfless and unconditional manner.

> But love your enemies, and do good, and lend, expecting nothing in return, and your reward will be great, and you will be sons of the Most High, for He is kind to the ungrateful and the evil (Luke 6:35).

When we express our love for others we also express our love for God. And through this act, we show others the God within us.

Suggested Prayer:

God, help me to love others as you have loved me. Let my love be unconditional and affirming. Let my love serve as a testimony of your presence within me.

Additional Biblical References:

1 John 4:12 No one has ever seen God; but if we love one another, God lives in us and his love is made complete in us.

John 13:35 By this all people will know that you are my disciples, if you have love for one another.

1 Corinthians 13:13 And now faith, hope, and love abide, these three; and the greatest of these is love.

BIBLICAL MEDITATION
Conclusion

Congratulations on completing STAND ON GRACE: 28 Days of Biblical Meditation! Whether it took 28 days or significantly longer – you started on, or continued upon, the path of establishing a true spiritual experience with God. You took steps to understand and fully implement His plans for your life.

This is a tremendous journey!

You will notice we began STAND ON GRACE: 28 Days of Biblical Meditation by contemplating the topic of fear and its presence in our lives. Fear is the biggest impediment to leading the extraordinary and impactful life that God calls us to lead. It is one of, if not the biggest, obstacles in our relationships with God and others.

Remember, we are commanded to "fear not" many times throughout the Bible.

The solution to fear is love. Thus, it is no coincidence that we end STAND ON GRACE: 28 Days of Biblical Meditation with the topic of love.

Love, is the beginning and root of all things. Love empowers us to surmount obstacles. Love allows us to develop into our full potential. Love allows us to fully experience and give gratitude to our Creator. Love allows us to be a reflection of God that others may see.

There is nothing greater than love. There is nothing we cannot do when we are guided by love. Though, it has been referenced several times throughout STAND ON GRACE, it bears repeating

> Love is patient, love is kind. It does not envy, it does not boast, it is not proud. It does not dishonor others, it is not self-seeking, it is not easily angered, it keeps no record of wrongs. Love does not delight in evil but rejoices with the truth. It always protects, always trusts, always hopes, always perseveres. Love never fails. And now these three remain: faith, hope and love. But the greatest of these is love (1 Corinthians 13:4-8,13).

When we express love as God has taught us we reflect His grace. When, we use the gifts and talents with which he has blessed us we make a tremendous impact in our world and in the lives of others. Love exposes wrongdoing and overcomes injustice.

This world is challenging and complicated. Often it is confusing. Yet, His Truth is absolute and based in love. We receive God's grace because we are loved. God's love offers us salvation.

We can stand on love.

We can **STAND ON GRACE.**

BIBLICAL MEDITATION

About the Author

Multilingual. Internationally Published. Recipient of Prestigious Degrees & Awards From Numerous National And International Institutions & Organizations

Ava R. Williams was an avid reader as a young child. Reading transported her far beyond her small backyard in Detroit, Michigan and instilled within her a desire to not only to explore the world but to make a positive and lasting difference as well. As a result of this desire, Ava speaks five languages and has accumulated a plethora of international experience.

Ava R. Williams is a member of many honor societies and has received numerous prestigious awards and scholarships including a Fulbright and Rotary Ambassadorial Scholarship. She has studied numerous times in Austria, Brazil, Estonia, France and Germany. Her undergraduate work was completed at the University of Notre Dame where she received a Bachelor's of Art in Political Science and German. Additionally, she received a diplôme from l'Institut des Etudes Politiques et Sociales (Sciences-Po) as well as a Master's degree in Social Policy from the Federal University of Espirito Santo (UFES) in Vitoria, Brazil.

Ava has applied for and received grants, founded and implemented nonprofit national and international projects and programs, worked with diverse populations, presented research, conducted business and published a variety of literary works in several foreign languages.

Ava founded PEI Consulting, a leading global professional services company that helps individuals, businesses and organizations maximize their success and make a meaningful impact.

Ava R. Williams is deeply committed to affecting positive and lasting change and empowering others to do so as well. Ava has served on the Notre Dame Club of Detroit Board of Directors, the Professional Plaza Clinics Board of Directors and the Wayne State Center for Peace and Conflict Community Friends

Committee. Ava's previous leadership activities also include: creating a scholarship fund in memory of community activist Rosalind Caldwell-Jones; leading an international campaign to find a bone marrow donor for Ludmila Albertasse, a journalist and social worker in Vitoria, Brazil; implementing nonprofit programs and activities in Vitoria, Brazil and Detroit, Michigan.

Ava is also the Executive Director and Founder of the PREMBEL Foundation which she officially launched in 2013. Among its list of accomplishments the PREMBEL foundation has: provided supplemental language, leadership and cultural services and activities to schools, groups and organizations in academically under-performing and/or economically disadvantaged areas; collaborated with local businesses and organizations to promote literacy via the International Storytelling Hour; partnered with local dance studios to promote culture and leadership via the International Leadership & Dance Program; worked with nonprofits promoting STEM; led service projects and arranged for the donation of needed materials to support environmental and conservation efforts in conjunction in with National Day of Service; and more.

The ideas, insights and experiences Ava has gained have enabled her to deliver dynamic inspirational information filled talks and presentations in the areas of Development & Success, Leadership Development, Academic Success & Preparation, Travel, Philanthropy, Inspiration and Spirituality to audiences worldwide.

Has God's grace transformed you? Do you have a personal experience or example to share regarding how one of the topics covered in STAND ON GRACE: 28 Days of Biblical Meditation has impacted or been expressed in your life? If so, we'd love to hear from you! Share your story at:

AlwaysStandOnGrace@gmail.com

Available In Audiobook Format

Discover The Joy of God's Transformative Grace Within You!

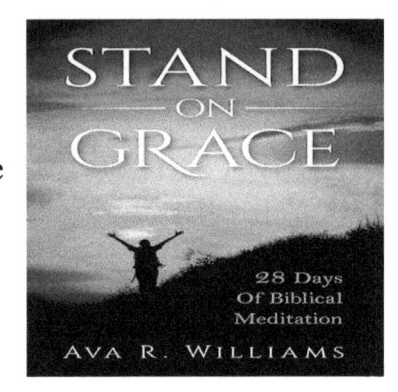

Want to learn how to better hear what God desires of, and for, you? The audiobook version of STAND ON GRACE: 28 Days of Biblical Meditation is the perfect guide to help you learn. Narrated by the author, Ava R. Williams, you'll learn about the ancient practice utilized by a myriad of biblical and historical figures and how it's principles can be directly applied to your life. Available for purchase at major retailers such as www.Amazon.com, via YWNL publishing or at www.AvaRWilliams.com.

Also Available in E-Book Format!

We hope you enjoyed this product from YWNL Publishing. Our goal is to provide inspirational and thought provoking books and products of the highest quality that highlight the world's many wonders and your potential to make it a better place. For information on additional YWNL books and products please contact:

YWNLpublishing@gmail.com
www.YWNLpublishing.com